Supporting Teachers
Supporting Pupils

This book draws from the real-life experiences and perceptions of secondary school teachers, and documents their ideas on how they define their job, the difficulties they face in the classroom and the support they need. Different approaches to teacher support are considered and the book includes an in-depth case study of a school that tried to implement some of these approaches. Key issues covered include:

- The motivations and needs of teachers and pupils
- The gaps between theory and practice in the professional role and performance of the teacher
- The behaviour of pupils and their views on the classroom
- Working with support staff
- The Assertive Discipline System

Drawing on her own experience and the experiences of others, Diana Fox Wilson recommends that all teachers are supported by a classroom environment that fosters insight and understanding between pupils and teachers, and urges a culture of change that recognises teachers as a crucial influence on young people's lives.

Supporting Teachers Supporting Pupils is packed with helpful and practical advice for all teachers. It will be a reassuring read for any teacher finding themselves feeling stranded in the classroom.

Diana Fox Wilson has spent many years working as a secondary school teacher, a teacher trainer and an education social worker.

Supporting Teachers Supporting Pupils

The emotions of teaching and learning

Diana Fox Wilson

RoutledgeFalmer
Taylor & Francis Group

LONDON AND NEW YORK

First published 2004
by RoutledgeFalmer
11 New Fetter Lane, London EC4P 4EE

Simultaneously published in the USA and Canada
by RoutledgeFalmer
29 West 35th Street, New York, NY 10001

Transferred to Digital Printing 2007

Routledge is an imprint of the Taylor & Francis Group, an informa business

Typeset in Baskerville by BC Typesetting Ltd, Bristol
Printed and bound in Great Britain by
TJI Digital, Padstow, Cornwall

British Library Cataloguing in Publication Data
A catalogue record for this book is available from the British Library

Library of Congress Cataloging in Publication Data
A catalog record for this book has been requested

ISBN 10: 0-415-33522-1 (hbk)
ISBN 10: 0-415-33523-X (pbk)

ISBN 13: 978-0-415-33522-5 (hbk)
ISBN 13: 978-0-415-33523-2 (pbk)

To Eastbank teachers and pupils and to teachers everywhere

Contents

Acknowledgements

My thanks are due to David Fulton, publisher, for permission to quote from Baker and Sikora (1982), included in Hanko, G. (1995) *Special Needs in Ordinary Classrooms*, London, David Fulton; and to Professor Brahm Norwich for permission to quote from the unpublished research report: Creese, A., Norwich, B. and Daniels, H. (1997a) 'Provision of a teacher-centred strategy for implementing the Code of Practice', Institute of Education, University of London.

My thanks also go to the editorial staff at Kogan Page and later at Routledge who have helped me to bring this book into being.

Above all, I want to thank the staff and former pupils of Eastbank school for their encouragement and patient collaboration, and the insights they gave me.

Introduction

This emotional business

Perhaps our biggest failure with student teachers is in not preparing them adequately for the emotional pressures on them and for the way their own emotional responses will help determine their reactions and behaviour in the classroom. However much I was able to analyse the situation – and this did help to neutralize my subjective reactions to a considerable extent – I could not always repress the rage, frustration, hurt, resentment, anxiety and insecurity I began to feel, particularly as my more rational, deliberately thought out strategies continued to fail – and inevitably my emotional responses began to colour my attitudes and interactions, so that I became apparently repressive, intolerant, inconsistent, overreacting, sarcastic, petty and defensive.

(Personal professional diary, quoted in Wilson, 2001, p 97)

Teaching is an emotional business.

(Student teacher [1995], unpublished research,
Leeds Metropolitan University)

This book is about the emotional business of teaching and learning. It shows how emotional needs may distort the interactions of both teachers and learners, and it discusses the kinds of support that teachers say they need to enable them to be the teachers they want to be. It proposes a return to a humanistic view of teaching which sees teachers as a crucial influence on young people's lives, and recommends that teachers are supported in establishing a classroom ethos in which they can respond with insight and understanding to pupils' needs. It is based on the premise, supported by my research into secondary school teaching, that teachers want not only to promote learning in their own subject but to help and guide pupils in the business of growing up.

The stereotypical image of good teachers is of confident, self-controlled and mature individuals who are able to leave their own personal problems at the school gates in order to address the personal problems of pupils. They conduct well-prepared, inspirational lessons, with tasks carefully graded to suit the heterogeneous needs of the class, and control with a light touch, derived from excellent organization and an appreciation of each pupil's intellectual and emotional needs. When behaviour problems do arise, these are dealt with calmly but firmly without fuss and the lesson continues with little interruption. Good teachers never resort to physical compulsion or punishment, never shout, except, occasionally, for deliberate effect, never respond to an individual pupil's behaviour, however offensive, with personal attack. Whatever their own emotions they keep them firmly in check. They are expected to be fully responsible for the class and to seek help only in the most extreme of emergencies. Failure to control a class or frequency of requests for help is regarded by colleagues, management and the educational establishment as a mark of incompetence and increasingly schools and local authorities are being urged to dismiss incompetent teachers.

Teachers in my own research (Wilson, 2001) noted the appearance of this 'super teacher' in the educational establishment's conception of the teacher's role, and recoiled from it. However desirable such an ideal, the impossibility of its realization merely depressed and demoralized. The attempt to meet such unrealistic standards is likely to increase teachers' feelings of failure, inadequacy and stress, and add to the negative emotional climate of the classroom.

Carlyle and Woods (2002) have movingly portrayed how the stress teachers are currently experiencing (through the massive and continuous reorganization that the education system has been undergoing in the past three decades) spills over into domestic life and back into their relationships with colleagues and pupils. I look in detail at the stress caused to teachers through their inability to be the teachers they want to be, and at the effects of this stress on their classroom relationships. Pupils also show signs of conflict between the pupil they want to be to fit in with teachers' and parents' expectations and the person their friends want them to be. The combined stress of teachers and pupils sometimes makes for explosive classrooms. This book maintains that:

- Teachers want to behave humanistically towards pupils, treating them with respect and understanding.
- Pupils want teachers to behave humanistically towards them.
- The emotional space for humanistic relations is often lacking in today's classrooms.
- Teachers and pupils experience conflict between the person they want to project and the person they are often perceived to be in the situation they are in.
- This internal conflict sometimes erupts in interpersonal conflict.
- Teachers cannot be expected to manage the emotional climate of the classroom on their own.
- Schools need to be organized to support teachers in creating classrooms in which both teachers and pupils can behave towards each other from the best of their humanity.

- Support initiatives that are imposed on teachers without taking into consideration teachers' own perceptions of their needs and that ignore the emotional component in classroom relationships are unlikely to have lasting effect.

Teaching – a humanistic endeavour

What do I mean when I talk about a 'humanistic' conception of the teacher's role? I regard the teaching of children and young people to take on adult roles in complex human societies as being one of the most important functions in a civilized community. Whatever its biological and social roots in our distant ancestry, the human species has extended the activity of passing on the collective culture of the human race and preparing the young for life in an increasingly complex and changing world to a significance far beyond the teaching and learning activities carried out in the rest of the animal kingdom. The *Concise Oxford Dictionary* gives as its second meaning of the word humanism 'a belief or outlook emphasizing common human needs and seeking only rational ways of solving human problems and concerned with humankind as responsible and progressive human beings'. One of our most powerful tools in the rational solving of problems is our ability to *communicate* in the widest sense of the word: to listen, understand, discuss, negotiate, compromise and collaborate. A humanistic view of teaching, therefore, puts a high value on the skills of communication, both those of the teacher, and those that it is our task to develop in the young.

However, rationality used to imply a conflict between reason and emotion in which the emotions were seen as obstructing a proper solution of problems and needed to be suppressed. The result of this suppression may well be stress, distorted perceptions and inappropriate reactions to situations. The recent work on emotional intelligence, popularized by Daniel Goleman (1995, 1998), suggests that we need to take our emotions, and other people's, seriously, and train them to contribute to the constructive solutions to problems.

Much of this book will be about emotions: the emotions that, if frustrated, too often distort our classroom relationships. I shall demonstrate that negative emotion often gets in the way of the rational, considered, humanistic responses. As I said earlier, the teacher's emotions are supposed to have no place in the classroom. I shall argue that, on the contrary, emotions are at the heart of the teaching–learning relationship, and, far from needing to banish emotion from the classroom, our task is to ensure a positive emotional climate. In considering the classroom from both the teacher's and the pupil's perspectives in Part I of the book, I explore some of the components, positive and negative, of the emotional maelstrom out of which teaching–learning relationships are formed. Teacher support may be seen in this context to consist in those attitudes, structures and provisions that encourage a benign emotional climate.

As long ago as 1979, Woods argued that the increasingly bureaucratic organization of secondary schools, which institutionalized the divisions of purposes between teachers, parents and pupils, acted against constructive personal relationships between pupils and teachers. More recent research and teachers' own experience suggests that schools have become even more bureaucratic, the conflicts more open and the climate even less favourable for schools trying to foster a humanistic ethos. This book looks at the emotional effect on both teachers and pupils of this thwarting of positive human relationships and its impact on classroom interaction. I examine some of the support measures that may help to counteract the pressures for conflict, and allow teachers and pupils to behave more constructively and with greater humanity towards one another.

However it is not my intention to imply that there are systems or strategies that, if followed to the letter, will bring about harmonious classrooms. This is not intended to be a how-to-do-it textbook on teacher support. Teaching and learning relationships, like all human interactions, are more complex than most systems of 'support' imply and simply do not always proceed as we want them to. What works in one set of circumstances may well not work in another. My intention has been to raise awareness of some of the emotional processes at work in the classroom, which people are often too embroiled in to see clearly. The support measures I examine are not to be interpreted as a blueprint, but as a means of highlighting the issues that need to be addressed. Every member of staff, from the bottom up, should be involved in discussing their own support needs and evolving their own structures.

The recent debate over the deployment of classroom support assistants reminded me forcibly of the lack of wisdom in trying to make broad generalizations. Based on my research fieldwork findings, I have suggested that classroom support assistants are welcomed and appreciated in mainstream classrooms. In the school where I conducted my fieldwork, adult support, whether from support teachers or classroom assistants, was one of the provisions that class teachers found most helpful and wanted to see extended. Yet there is clearly a difference of opinion voiced in the media and by the teaching unions about the increased employment of unqualified staff, and their precise role. My research suggests that inflexible demarcations of roles and responsibilities are unwise. The effectiveness of the support offered by classroom assistants is likely to depend on the personalities, perceptions, attitudes and ways of interacting of both teachers and assistants, and on the time committed to liaising and joint planning. With regard to support initiatives in general, the quality of the relationships that have been allowed to develop and flourish in an institution may well be the most important factor in determining what works or not. The initiatives described in this book, while not claiming to have all the answers, are intended to raise questions amongst practitioners about the issues involved and suggest important lines of development.

The origin of the book

In January 1988, I returned to secondary comprehensive school teaching after many years of working in other capacities within the education service. The shock to my professional ideals and value systems when I came up against resistant and rebellious youth and a reactionary and unsupportive school structure drove me to near despair and to serious distortion of my teaching practices and behaviour towards pupils. Although I changed schools twice, the damage to my self-concept as a human being and as a professional was never healed. I became angry that committed professionals, prepared to be as hard-working, imaginative, self-critical and flexible as I was, and as many of my colleagues were, could be allowed by the system to become so destroyed and destructive.

In 1994, therefore, I took early retirement and embarked on an exploration of teacher support. From the first, the research was carried out on behalf of teachers and with the fullest collaboration from them that their overloaded and stressed lives would permit. It is a logical necessity that the implications of that research for the organization of schools and the practice of teaching should be more widely available to the profession. This book is therefore grounded in the research but focuses more directly on the significance of its findings and their possible application in schools than did the original study.

The research, and hence the book, arose out of direct personal experience of stress within the profession, backed up by several contemporary investigations (Dunham, 1992; Travers and Cooper, 1996; Woods *et al*, 1997). Stress has been shown to have been increasing over the past three decades because of, amongst other things, the rate of change in the profession and subsequent intensification of teachers' work (A Hargreaves, 1994), political, media and public perceptions of teachers, and the imposed changes in their professional role (Niaz, 1989; Woods *et al*, 1997) and teachers' own perceptions and experience of increasing disaffection and disruption amongst pupils (Elton, 1989). The increase in stress amongst teachers has led in turn to an increase in long-term sickness, early exit from the profession and difficulties in recruiting teachers in the first place – all now well documented (Travers and Cooper, 1996; Carlyle and Woods, 2002). What has only recently been explored is the emotional fallout of all this stress on individual teachers and the distorting effect it has on their relationships with pupils, colleagues and family (Wilson, 2001; Carlyle and Woods, 2002). This book looks particularly at the stress surrounding teachers' and pupils' classroom relationships, the emotions generated, the distortions of behaviour occasioned and the nature of the support needed to allow teachers to operate in a sane environment according to their own professional values and purposes.

An emotional odyssey

The origin of the research that underpins this book was my own emotional experience of teaching. On one level, I used the research to distance myself from events and to analyse the processes that were taking place. I have used anecdotes from this experience that sometimes do not portray me in a favourable light as a teacher, and that even now are painful to remember. I have done this deliberately. When teachers lose control of themselves and the pupils, it is a shaming event. They think they have offended against two of the qualities that make them into teachers: the ability to manage a large group of children or young people, and the presentation of themselves as role models for rational, considered behaviour. Teachers take a pride in successfully controlling classes, and are sometimes less than sympathetic to those who fail. Consequently, unless teachers have a supportive group of colleagues or a departmental management in whom they have confidence, they tend to keep their failures to themselves if they can.

I do not wish to imply that teachers are losing control of themselves in large numbers, screaming at pupils or hitting them. Incidents that I know of are few and mainly anecdotal, and do not relate specifically to the fieldwork school. However, there were considerable indications that teachers found themselves acting in ways that distorted them as human beings. Because of the pressures on them, both from pupils' behaviour and from the external demands placed on them, they were aware of responding to incidents inappropriately, in ways that exacerbated rather than calmed a situation, and the cumulative frustration of not being the person they wanted to be was having a destructive effect on morale and motivation.

It is my conviction that critical incidents need to be brought out into the open in an atmosphere of trust and goodwill, so that lessons can be learnt from them at all levels. However, the anecdotes I have used from my own experience are not there for the sake of self-revelation. They are carefully chosen to back up or illustrate the points I am making in the text, which are based on the research. So often teachers are given advice by experts or 'model teachers', which throws into relief their own imperfections, and makes them feel more of a failure than they really are. Sometimes they need to know that others experience the same difficulties as they do. Then they can collectively do something about it.

The concept of teacher support

At the time that I began my research, the concept of teacher support and related terms – support for teachers, a supportive ethos – were beginning to appear in the literature without any clear agreement about what the term implied and what constituted support. The literature divided roughly into two main categories: initiatives that aimed the support at the teacher and the teacher's practices and those that aimed to support the pupil. Cutting across these two categories were two more: the literature of support for pupils with special educational needs and the literature of support to regulate pupil behaviour. All these studies tended to focus on specific projects that aimed to offer rational solutions to problems of pupil learning and behaviour but did not address the immediate problems of classroom encounters and the emotions generated. The recommended approaches to teacher support were devised externally and imposed on teachers from outside. They did not take into account teachers' own perceptions of their support needs.

The research that underpins this book set out to explore the concept of support from the point of view of teachers' perceptions of their classroom needs and the kinds of support that would address those needs. It is an in-depth study in one school, backed up by my own teaching experience across three secondary comprehensive schools. Since I completed my field-work, other research with different foci of interest is now reinforcing the insights I gained into the emotional interactions of both teachers and pupils (Coldron, 2002; Carlyle and Woods, 2002). My findings are therefore part of a growing body of research that emphasizes the importance of a supportive classroom climate for the well-being of both teachers and pupils and there-fore for effective teaching and learning.

My research comprised two main sources of data. Firstly, I subjected my own personal professional diaries, kept over seven years across three different schools, to an in-depth analysis that furnished me with experiential evidence of the kinds of situations for which I had felt the need for support. The methodological reasons for the use of such personal material were argued in the original thesis. This was then placed alongside the evidence derived from the fieldwork and the research literature as a means of gaining a more complete emotional picture. The conclusions that I draw on to provide the themes of this book derive from the fieldwork. But I also use quotations from my own diaries where these substantiate and illuminate the point I wish to make.

The fieldwork took the form of an in-depth study in a single school over one year and two terms. This consisted of unstructured interviews, informal discussion, lesson observation, both as an objective observer and as a partici-pant in the role of support teacher, informal observation in the staffroom and in meetings. The interviews involved 30 members of staff, including class teachers, members of middle and senior management, support staff and student teachers. The informal conversations involved many more. The interviews were recorded and the transcripts returned to the participants for comment and amendment. The informal discussions were summarized in my research journal and copies given to participants for comment. At several points during the period of the fieldwork I summarized findings and issues for comment by the participants. In this way I tried to ensure that the con-clusions I reached represented a consensus of opinion. Sixteen pupils were also interviewed either informally as individuals or during more structured group discussions. Their contributions, reinforced by pupils' remarks and opinions recorded in my diaries, furnished me with insights into pupils' perceptions of their own needs.

Eastbank School – a pen portrait

In 1995, when I embarked on the fieldwork, Eastbank School was a maintained 11 to 16, mixed comprehensive school of around 1,200 pupils, situated in a traditionally working class area of a city which has lost most of its former industrial base and was putting much effort into presenting a new image to the world. Nevertheless, older forms of employment have been lost to the pupils who attend Eastbank School, and new opportunities and new conceptions of the future develop only slowly. The traditional catchment area consists of terraces of small owner-occupied houses, a sizable council estate, and some new private housing, but it was the perception of staff in the school at the time of the research that government legislation on open enrolment had led to increased skewing of the intake towards the lower end of the social scale and ability range. The percentage of pupils on free school meals was 27.4; the number of statemented pupils was 20; the percentage of year seven pupils requiring learning support in English through withdrawal for one or two lessons per week was 19.75 (1995–96 percentages). Pupils of Afro-Caribbean or Asian origin are very rare in the school, but it takes a growing number of children from traveller families and specialist staff are available to meet their specific needs. Again, it was a widespread perception of the staff in the school at the time that pupils' behaviour in classrooms and around the school had been deteriorating, and the job of managing classrooms and teaching effectively was becoming more difficult.

The head teacher of the school had been appointed several years previously to steer the school through a fundamental reorganization of the local authority's schools, which was experienced by many teachers as profoundly stressful. During 1995–96, the year of my main fieldwork in the school, a general OFSTED inspection of the school took place. The school was placed under special measures, the head teacher retired in 1997 and a further OFSTED inspection took place in 1998 during the time of my follow up fieldwork. The school was removed from special measures, but the preparation for and experience of the OFSTED visits and the trauma of the intervening two years imposed considerable pressures on staff, and may well have had a distorting effect on their work and on their own perceptions of their needs. Eastbank School is a pseudonym and today, in 2003, is a very different place from the school I knew in 1996. There have been changes in management and personnel, to the curriculum and to pastoral care and teacher support structures. Many of the contributors to this book are no longer at the school. So, to all intents and purposes Eastbank School does not exist, but may serve as a metaphor for secondary comprehensive schools up and down the country.

In common with all state schools, Eastbank School has also been faced with the upheavals and challenges of the National Curriculum and associated target-setting and system of assessment. All of these have contributed to the turbulence and insecurity experienced by staff and pupils in Eastbank as in most other schools, the effects of which on teacher morale and well-being have been well documented (Woods *et al*, 1997; Carlyle and Woods, 2002). Teachers I interviewed described their experience of their work at this time in metaphors that referred to drowning, being engulfed; or to juggling too many plates or balls, and no longer feeling in control of them. There is a need to ask questions about the effect these feelings of powerlessness must be having on the classroom life of teacher and pupils, and what support is needed not just to keep them afloat but to allow them to continue to prosper. These are questions this book sets out to address.

The structure of the book

The book is in three parts. It is designed to be either read in its entirety, or, given the term-time pressures on teachers, to allow them to focus on specific chapters. This has entailed some repetition of important points from chapter to chapter, to retain context and continuity. Part I looks at classroom interaction from the points of view of both teachers and pupils and reveals similarities in the nature of the frustrations and conflicts that each experience and that often sabotage classroom relationships. It also suggests that both teachers and pupils want the same kind of classroom, one that is free of 'hassle', where they can work constructively and collaboratively.

Part II describes several initiatives introduced into Eastbank School to support both teachers and pupils and evaluates these against the criteria for support suggested in Part I. These include: a whole school behavioural system; the use of extra adults in the classroom; collaborative and peer support initiatives; forms of professional development; the role of the staff tutor. Where appropriate, examples are also given from the research literature and from other schools. I argue throughout the section that initiatives based on the purely rational model, which claims that if teachers behave in specific ways, pupils will also behave appropriately, fail to address the non-rational causes of much classroom conflict. Moreover, the success of support initiatives depends largely on the attitudes to teachers that underpin them and the priority in terms of time and status that the school is prepared to give them.

Part III makes the argument, based on the evidence revealed in the preceding chapters, for a conception of teaching and learning that centres around the crucial relationship between adults and children, and emphasizes the role of the human qualities of respect, communication, imagination and empathy. In particular, it highlights the importance that both teachers and pupils placed on the role of talk, discussion, explanation and the non-verbal communication skills of expressing pleasure, praise and understanding.

It stresses the complex nature of the teaching and learning processes and the role, both positive and negative, played by the emotions; and explores how individual teachers' personal and professional values and teaching purposes might be accommodated. It argues for a view of classroom relationships, based not on conflict and authoritarian control, but on willing cooperation and collaboration. Support is defined as those attitudes, provisions and strategies that would enable teachers to function within such a conception of a collaborative classroom and according to their own professional objectives.

Part I

What are we here for?

1 Entertainers, gurus and mentors

Teachers' perspectives

I think that I would expect from above, from the hierarchy, the adminis-
tration, a structure in which a reasonably competent, civilized person
could perform the function that they're supposed to perform . . . I think
an average person with average ability and good faith should be able to
walk into most classrooms and teach. So I want a framework that
allows me to do that.

(Teacher, Wilson, 2001)

Posing the right questions

When teachers say, as most of them have said at one time or another, 'I need
support', what is meant by it? In a fraught classroom with 9D, it may mean:

There is nothing more I can do with this class at this moment. They are
neither interested in the activities I so imaginatively dreamt up for
them nor the materials I spent hours last night lovingly creating. They
have become bored and restless. They are trying to derive a little fun
out of winding me up, and because I am exhausted and frustrated,
conscious of the noise spilling out from my classroom and feeling very
vulnerable, they will probably succeed. Any moment now I shall blow
my top. I need support, but if I ask for it, I am admitting failure.

Or on another occasion:

Darren is starting again. I have just launched into my introductory
presentation of the new topic, the presentation that I have carefully prepared to be as motivating and involving as possible, and he has already
set about sabotaging my lesson. He begins by asking for a pen. I say he
doesn't need it yet, but I give it anyway to save argument. I continue
with my presentation. He says the pen doesn't work. I say could he put
his pen down please, and just listen. He says it's boring, why should he
listen, it's a waste of time. I ignore that and continue. He says audibly
enough for me to overhear, 'The silly cow won't give me a pen that

works.' I try to ignore this too. But I feel the anger welling up inside me. I tell myself about all his problems, his need for attention, his need to look hard.

A few seconds later a pen flies across the room towards me from somewhere in his direction. The excitement in the room is palpable. The rest of the class is waiting to see what I will do. If I send him outside into the corridor, he will continue to disrupt, and other people's lessons as well as mine. If I send him to the head of department next door, that will interrupt her lesson as well and it will be another black mark against me. I can put him in detention, but that won't solve the immediate situation, and he probably wouldn't turn up for detention anyway, so I'd have to spend time chasing him up. 'Stay behind at the end of the lesson, Darren', I say. 'You see', he says to the rest of the class, 'she's blaming me as usual. It wasn't me.'

I'm beginning to panic. 'Shut up', I say, seeing the lesson slipping away from me, 'we'll talk about that at the end of the lesson.' He shuts up temporarily, but it's too late. The pupils have lost concentration. The presentation is ruined. I put a ready prepared piece of work on the overhead projector and tell them to copy it into their books. A gobbet of spit lands on my jumper. I crack. I march up to him and, big though he is, I manhandle him roughly out of the room, tearing his shirt collar in the process, to the delight of the rest of the class. He stalks off down the corridor shouting that I'm for it now. Heads look out from the surrounding classrooms. Somewhere along the way of that disastrous lesson, I needed support.

These are fictitious examples constructed out of elements of real incidents but they follow a pattern familiar to me and to countless other teachers, I am sure. They show situations, not of lazy, uncommitted, incompetent or bullying teachers who deserve the failed lessons, the derision of pupils, and the threat of disciplinary action. They portray ordinary teachers who try hard to be well prepared with motivating lessons; to understand the perspectives of pupils and the needs of individuals; who try to keep calm in the face of mounting provocation and personal attack and who end up providing routine copying activities to restore or maintain calm, or who snap and lose control of themselves as well as the class. What kinds of support might have prevented these fictitious lessons following the course they did?

A third scenario concerns a teacher who believes in teaching individually for most of the time. She spends a great deal of effort and imagination preparing individualized worksheets for the wide ability range in the class, in the conviction that the pupils' needs are best met in this way and control of the class is easier if they are engaged in tasks that offer them a sense of achievement. But reading and understanding the worksheets is not easy for some of the pupils, and while she is helping these, others become stuck and in need of help. The task of getting round the class giving the help that is needed *when* it is needed becomes overwhelming. The pupils become frustrated, bored and therefore mischievous, preventing others from working. The teacher blames herself for the pupils' disruption, thus adding to her own sense of stress and guilt.

The point about all these vignettes is that the teachers concerned are trying to be good professionals. They think about the needs of the subject, the pupils, the particular context of the lesson. When things go wrong, they tend to blame themselves: the lesson wasn't pitched right, the activities were not motivating enough, they handled this pupil wrongly, they did not foresee that situation, they should be able to control the class and themselves, they have not acted in accordance with their own teaching principles. They perceive, correctly or not, that colleagues will also blame them. The outcome of all this self-blame and feeling of failure is to create a snowball of stress so that the chances of similarly failed lessons in the future are increased.

Yet these teachers are theoretically amongst those that Chris Woodhead, Chief Inspector in the mid- to late 1990s, might have counted amongst his 4 per cent of incompetent teachers (Woodhead, 2002).

Difficulty in managing classrooms has traditionally been seen as one of the characteristics of failing teachers:

> There is also a minority of teachers, who, for a variety of reasons, cannot manage an orderly classroom, and who are judged by students and colleagues alike to be of doubtful competence. Most of these teachers survive; few are dismissed or guided into alternative employment. The measures for removing incompetent teachers are slow and complicated, demanding remarkable patience and skill from a complainant head teacher. Worse still, everybody in schools knows this is a problem that needs to be addressed, but are too embarrassed to do so openly.
>
> (D Hargreaves, 1994, p 8)

Yet few commentators on educational matters query the term 'incompetent' and bother to look at the values, motivations, commitment and sensitivities of those teachers so labelled. I shall argue throughout this book that:

- The way schools and teachers regard classroom management needs to change radically, from seeing it as the sole responsibility, and often a matter of pride, of the individual teacher, to seeing it as a collective responsibility of the school.
- Attitudes to teachers who 'appear' to be failing in keeping order need to change.
- Classroom disorder often arises from or is exacerbated by the conflict caused to both teacher and pupils when they find themselves acting 'out of character', that is, against the person they really want to be.

- In the pressures and complexities of today's classrooms, both teachers and pupils need support to act out of the best of themselves; to be fully human in the most positive sense of the word.

So what is meant by support? Throughout the book, I shall attempt to tease out teachers' support needs, and identify the kinds of support that best meet those needs. Underpinning these needs are the personal and professional values of teachers, and the kinds of teacher they want to be. The kinds of questions that need to be asked in relation to the three hypothetical situations described above are:

- What kind of teacher does this teacher want to be?
- What are her or his intentions for the lesson?
- What is preventing the teacher from fulfilling those intentions?
- What are the teacher's perceptions of what is going on?
- What are the pupils' perceptions of what is going on?
- What are the emotions generated in both teacher and pupils?
- What kinds of support might have allowed the lesson to proceed in the way the teacher had intended?
- What kinds of longer-term support might help the teacher make changes in the conduct of lessons, and his or her coping strategies?

'Needing support' is often talked about without properly defining exactly what it is in the situation that requires support, and what kinds of support would meet the needs of the situation. Support strategies in the literature tend to be devised by external experts to meet problems defined by the experts that do not necessarily reflect the problems as perceived by the practitioners. The assumption is that if teachers improve their lesson planning, delivery, choice of materials, relationships with pupils and handling of inappropriate behaviour, all will be well. If only . . . There is little recognition that there are emotional dynamics in the teaching–learning situation that may sabotage the best efforts of the most committed teachers. In this book I hope to give some insight into these.

In the next section I draw on my research to explore how the teachers in my fieldwork school perceived the job of teaching in today's classroom, what brought them into teaching, what are the difficulties for which they feel the need for support and what kinds of support they need. I present teachers' ideal professional image – the kind of teacher they want to be – and reveal some of the barriers to fulfilling their professional ideals. I show how the emotional pressures of the classroom distort their professional behaviour and cause conflict between the professional self that teachers want to project and the way they are in fact being perceived. I suggest that the main function of support is to prevent or alleviate this experience of disjunction. What kind of support will allow teachers to be the teachers they want to be?

The teacher I want to be – the love triangle

> I came into teaching because I wanted pupils to enjoy [subject] like I
> enjoyed it at school. I wanted to give them that opportunity because I
> really enjoyed it, so why couldn't I just go and help somebody else to
> enjoy it as much as I did?
>
> (Student teacher, Wilson, 2001)

> When I started teaching, one of the things that I was expected to do was
> to give as much information and to educate and advise and support
> young people, and that was the sole purpose of my job. It was to go in
> there and do absolutely everything.
>
> (Teacher, Wilson, 2001)

The ways in which these secondary school teachers talked about their work
dispels the old distinction between primary and secondary school teaching –
the 'I teach children not subjects' dichotomy. This distinction was still being
asserted as recently as 2002 (Hodkinson at BERA conference, 2002). The
presenter of a conference paper maintained that secondary school teachers
saw themselves primarily as subject specialists, while primary school teachers
saw themselves as teachers. My research suggests that this is an oversimpli-
fication of a more complex relationship that secondary school teachers
have both with subject and with pupils. It is a triangular relationship, with
teachers often loving their subject and wanting to convey the beauty and
enjoyment of it to pupils. At the same time, they are aware of the intellectual,
emotional and social needs of pupils, and value the closer relationships with
them that have developed in the last few decades. They are concerned, not
only to teach their own subject in educationally valid and motivating ways,
but to do this in ways that take into account the specific needs of individuals.
With regard to the pupils in this triangle, the aim is that they should be
inspired and influenced by the teacher to understand and appreciate the
subject area, and eventually become independent learners.

This makes teachers vulnerable on two counts: the subject and the relationship. Failure to communicate the subject matter in motivating and intel-
lectually valid ways causes frustration to the teacher and boredom to the
pupil. Failure to respond appropriately to the needs of pupils arouses resentment, hostility and alienation in *them*, and guilt and defensiveness in the
teacher. Either way, pupils are turned off the subject and teachers feel
demoralized. It is necessary to look more closely at the things that can go
wrong in both the subject and relationship dimensions of the triangle and at
the kinds of support that teachers need to fulfil both teaching objectives.

Recognition of the importance of both objectives does not imply that all
teachers feel they have equal competence in or propensity for both. All the
teachers I spoke with recognized that motivating and effective communication of subject involved responding to pupils' individual needs, but some

expressed a preference for the teaching of the subject over a more explicit pastoral role, while others were increasingly drawn by choice into pastoral responsibilities. Clearly, supporting teachers will involve recognizing and taking account of these individual differences in their skills and aptitudes:

> I have always thought of school as being primarily academic, and that the social side of it should have remained part of the hidden curriculum, a very important part but nevertheless hidden; and I resented the formalization of what people of my generation always saw as the accepted but undefined curriculum . . . and in that sense I would have accepted the changes if the people directing the changes had recognized the talents and beliefs, for want of a better word, of people like myself, and said there was room for people like me . . . as well as those who saw their role in the wider sense of pastoral care for children; and I feel strongly that there is room for both in schools.
>
> (Teacher, Wilson, 2001)

The teacher as subject communicator

> I decided that I wanted to teach [subject] because I really like it as a subject, and I think a lot of people should like it, but they don't . . . I'm trying to get people to understand it a bit more. I mean, it is a beautiful subject.
>
> (Student teacher, Wilson, 2001)

> But I do enjoy teaching [subject]. It's good fun. Yes I enjoy teaching because most of the time we're doing [aspect of subject] at the moment, which admittedly I prefer, and they enjoy it. They enjoy doing that sort of thing.
>
> (Teacher, Wilson, 2001)

These teachers had come into teaching because of their own love of their subject and their desire to communicate this love to children; and they were prepared to put much effort into achieving this. They talk about enjoyment and sharing, about enthusiasm and the buzz that comes from perceiving that pupils have understood something they did not know before. Imagery taken from the fields of entertainment and the arts abounds (see p. 28). Some teachers talk about the beauty of their subject, and teach with almost messianic fervour. Many wanted lessons to be fun for both the pupils and themselves. Two talk about the aesthetic and humanistic value of knowledge for its own sake, irrespective of its economic benefits. One speaks of the enthusiasm with which she follows developments in the teaching of her subject. One mentions the satisfaction that achievement in her subject brings to less academic pupils.

There was also much talk about the frustrations involved in teaching particular subjects. Several teachers felt that the requirements of the National Curriculum in their subject were inappropriate to the needs of many of their pupils; and the system no longer allowed them the flexibility to match the content and teaching strategies to their own teaching contexts.

This caused teachers much frustration and guilt because they perceived that pupils' behaviour was deteriorating because of their boredom and alienation from the subject:

> [expanding on a remark to do with stress] . . . because of the fact that we have to deliver a curriculum and we can't move. We have to deliver it according to schemes of work, and kids fail because they have no experience of it. They have nothing to base their work on. They find that they are easily distracted. Because the kids fail they misbehave, which interferes with other kids and it has a knock on effect.
>
> (Teacher, Wilson, 2001)

Keeping pupils on task was a constant source of hassle and irritation, which interrupted the flow of the lesson and affected the concentration of other pupils as well as the disrupters. Teachers gave examples of the kinds of behaviours they had to contend with. They talked of the girl who's just a 'little natter-pants', the 'little boy behaviours' like throwing screwed up bits of paper across the room, or continually opening and closing drawers. But they also described incidents of more confrontational, personally insulting or threatening behaviour: the flat refusal to obey an instruction, the deliberate gross interruption of a lesson to draw attention to themselves, the sotto voce or open swearing at the teacher, the throwing of coins and hard sweets at the teacher.

Past research (Kyriakou, 1989; Elton, 1989) has suggested that what teachers find most stressful about pupils' classroom behaviour is the difficulty of getting them to do any work, and my research suggests that the hurt teachers feel at the more personally directed behaviours arises from the implied rejection of them in their teacher's role, because it is also a rejection of the personal values and commitment on which that role is founded, and therefore a rejection of the teacher as a person. This rejection of the self is bound to arouse defensive and hostile emotions in the teacher, however able he or she is to intellectualize the causes of pupils' behaviour. As one teacher said, when her carefully prepared teaching materials were rejected out of hand, 'I could have killed them.' One of the tasks of support for teachers must be to help them work through the immediate emotional reaction in a constructive way and then to provide the opportunities for a more dispassionate analysis of the situation and more considered strategies.

At the same time as deploring the amount of sheer hassle and emotional effort involved in motivating pupils and encouraging sustained work, teachers also enjoyed the closer relationships with pupils that decades of a more child-centred approach to teaching had fostered, and were aware that traditional ways of managing classrooms and delivering lessons were no longer appropriate and were likely to antagonize today's young people: 'I certainly feel better being able to be approached more directly by children and being able to approach them, rather than standing at the front of a class delivering a lesson and walking out with a waft of a gown at the end of it like some of them used to do' (teacher, Wilson, 2001).

The teacher as tutor

One teacher said, 'I came into teaching with so many ideas about helping pupils' (Wilson, 2001).

Teachers used a lot of what I have termed 'service imagery' to characterize their relationships with pupils, the teacher–pupil arm of the triangle. Here, the focus is on the individual needs of each pupil, whether these are learning, emotional or social. There is a recognition that pupils' learning is affected by these needs, which must be responded to for effective learning to take place. This does not simply involve the teacher's response to pupils with recognized special educational needs, although, since the introduction of policies of greater integration of these children into mainstream classes, this takes up increasing amounts of teachers' time and thought in terms of materials and teaching approaches. It is a global attitude involving responding appropriately to all the idiosyncrasies of the individual learner; being aware of the specific circumstances that might be affecting pupils' responses at a particular time; divining the learning styles of individual pupils and keying into these. It means tuning in to the learner's wavelength. It involves intuiting how a particular pupil is construing a situation, empathizing with him or her and understanding the underlying reasons for specific behaviour; and it implies modifying one's response as a teacher and classroom manager to take these individual interpretations into account.

Teachers talked of creating and maintaining 'good relationships with pupils', 'teaching much of the time individually', 'listening' to pupils, 'helping individual pupils', giving 'individual attention'. The following is a telling description of an incident in which the teacher determined and modified her response to a particular girl in the light of her own knowledge of the girl's difficulties and motivations. It well illustrates teachers' conflicting responses to the needs of individual pupils and the whole group and the demands of the structured behavioural system the school followed at the time of the research:

> I have this girl in my group because she causes a lot of problems, but I get on alright with her, so she shouldn't really be in the top group but it causes less hassle if she's in the top group. She's dizzy, she's dozy, and it's 'Oh yes', and finally she'll cotton on 10 minutes later. And she was doing that and I was at the OHP and I was actually writing. We'd

started, and she decided she'd tidy her folder out, which was inappropriate behaviour at the wrong time. I ignored that because I was busy teaching, and then she went 'Pss! Over here!' I said, 'No [name].' I mean, really it shouldn't happen. It should be: write name on the board, and a cross [the staggered sanctions of the discipline system in use] . . . and eventually she came and dumped all the stuff she'd got in her folder.

She wasn't being naughty or horrible, she was doing something really good for her, she was tidying her folder out . . . and she dumped it all out on my desk. I told her she was extremely rude, and all this sort of thing, and she basically called me a bitch, because she is irascible. So she had to be sent to remove. I mean, that's the 'extreme clause' [sanction of removal from class provided for in the discipline system]. You can't have people calling you a bitch, right? But I felt so . . . in a way . . . I know she didn't mean it, but that's only because I know [girl's name]. It's because she blows her top, and she felt, really, she was doing something alright.

So she had to be sent to remove, and she should have been in remove the day after as well. Now she didn't actually get to remove because she was very upset about this, because she'd done it to little me, you know, and she actually went to see her house tutor, and came to see me at the end of the day and apologized. She was very sorry, she knew she'd been rude etcetera. She also told me that I shouldn't really have made her look small in front of the rest of the class. So we went through all this. We had this discussion. I did say, 'Well your punishment is that you're in remove tomorrow . . .' and overnight I thought, well she came actually on her own at the end of the day, not just at three-twenty, but at half past three, and did apologize nicely, and there was nothing to be gained at all by her being in remove for the rest of the day, out of all those lessons.

(Teacher, Wilson, 2001)

I have quoted this incident at length because it so graphically illustrates the complexities of the teaching–learning relationship: the many, sometimes conflicting factors teachers have to take account of in the split-second decisions they are often called upon to make in dealing with pupils' disruptive behaviour and the support needs of both teacher and pupils in such situations. It demonstrates how a situation can be interpreted in many different ways that call on incompatible solutions and the confrontation this can lead to without anyone really intending it. It shows the conflicting needs of the individual and the group, and the balancing act the teacher has to try to perform between the two. One can well imagine the frustration of the teacher firstly in trying to teach against the girl's demands for attention, and then in having to take the action required by the discipline system, while also understanding the girl's motivations. But this account also highlights the power of discussion and negotiation, and the need for the time and emotional space to allow this to happen.

The operative factors in this incident were:

- the individual needs of the girl in conflict with the needs of the whole class;
- the conflict within the teacher as she tries to meet both sets of needs;
- the growing emotional involvement of both teacher and pupil: the latter's need for the teacher's approval and her hurt and resentment when she thinks she isn't getting it, and the former's frustration at having to juggle the conflicting needs of both individual and group;
- the flash point that produces the pivotal confrontation;
- the sometimes inflexible requirements of the structured behavioural system conflicting with the teacher's professional assessment of the girl's needs;
- the time out facility, which allowed both girl and teacher a breathing space in which emotional response could be replaced by more considered understanding of each other's point of view.

Later, I shall consider the kinds of support teachers need to deal with situations like this. In preparation, you might like to take a few minutes considering what you might have done in this situation, and what additional support provisions might have helped.

Stress, insecurity and isolation

> When I started teaching . . . I could teach intuitively; I could teach off the top of my head; I had a curriculum I had to follow, but the ways I delivered that curriculum had to be according to my needs, and most of all the kids' needs. And those kids' needs were very varied and so I could vary the delivery. Now I have to deliver according to very narrow boundaries and I have to put it all down on paper before I deliver the curriculum. The curriculum has changed very much indeed, and I think because of that the quality of teaching is not as good as it was. I certainly don't think it's so good for me. I don't find it as satisfying, and I don't think I'm teaching as well as I used to because my boundaries are too small and the other work I do is too great. I actually think the quality of my work has gone down.
>
> (Teacher, Wilson, 2001)

It can be seen that teachers fundamentally have very positive feelings towards their work, involving enthusiasm for their subject and a desire to communicate both the understanding and the enthusiasm to others, and the creation and maintenance of good relationships with pupils through attempting to meet their individual needs. Even gross misbehaviour on the part of pupils is often met with an attempt to understand and respond to the reasons for that bad behaviour. This desire to see a situation from pupils' points of view and to give individual support springs from teachers' own deeply held personal and professional value systems and reasons for being in the profession.

However, there was ample evidence from the ways in which teachers talked, that these positive feelings were being eroded by elements in the contemporary condition of teaching that challenged their perceptions of who they were and why they were there. In particular, the sheer volume of demands, expectations and responsibilities on limited time; the barriers to successful teaching of the subject; the perceived deteriorating relationships with pupils who were not getting the attention they needed; and the accumulation of pressures on the teachers' self-confidence and morale were in many cases threatening to tip the balance between commitment and alienation:

> [explaining why she intends to retire early] . . . it's because it's a 24-hour stress system that I'm not prepared to jeopardize the health and the rest of my life with my husband [for]. I believe that teaching is much more stressful now than it's ever been. It's stressful because we have to jump through hoops we don't want to and the quality of our teaching could, I believe, be directly affected by the other things we have to do, and are expected to do, and because of the fact that our product that we work with has changed so much in the last 10 years that I don't want to stay in it because it's not the job I started doing.

> At the moment I'm spreading myself so thinly that I'm not doing anything properly. I mean, I'm a complete failure, and [it's] not really my fault, but that's just the circumstances. And it's getting to the point now where it's intolerable, really, you know, because you just never feel as if you're doing the job properly. I don't consider that I'm doing my job properly.
>
> (Teachers, Wilson, 2001)

I have already commented on the language teachers used in talking about their work as currently perceived. Teachers use imagery of drowning; of being overwhelmed; of being flattened, drained of themselves; of running around aimlessly like a headless chicken; of having to juggle too many balls or plates at once, to describe the experience of being overloaded with tasks and responsibilities. They talk about the continuous hassle with pupils; the apparent fruitlessness of many of their attempts to manage or teach them; of being worn down by petty irritations; of the frustration of having lessons sabotaged by the disruption of a minority; of the humiliations of being at the receiving end of personal insults or physical missiles from pupils. They talk about the guilt of knowing that much of the class disruption arises from their own failure to give the necessary personal attention. They sometimes feel that they are losing themselves, the person they know themselves to be, the teacher they want to be and are acting in ways quite at variance with their own professional standards. Some feel that the teaching profession has lost direction and changes in the teaching of their own subjects have diminished their relevance for pupils, or their academic validity: 'I could, if asked, give a very good case, a well-reasoned case to argue that education has taken a number of wrong turns . . . and I think that what's missing in teaching today: we're all teaching a curriculum and not teaching subjects . . .' (teacher, Wilson, 2001).

It is worth pausing to consider for a moment the effect that these experiences of being continuously buffeted by demands, expectations and hostility must have on teachers' nerves, on their psyche and sense of self. And their confidence is further eroded by the feelings of guilt that accompany their failure to teach and to relate to pupils in ways that accord with their personal and professional ideals. Disjunction, the awareness of the kind of person they are presenting to pupils and to colleagues, which differs profoundly from the person they know themselves to be by conviction, is a source of great distress to many teachers: 'I try to see the good in everybody. I came into teaching with so many ideas about helping pupils . . . As I see it, I've sunk to adopting strategies which are against my educational principles, and that creates conflict in me. I just seem to have to keep beating them down all the time' (teacher, Wilson, 2001).

Teachers sometimes try to operate in the classroom in a state of extreme emotional rawness, and it is not surprising that sensitivities, further inflamed through contact with the nervous excitability and emotional brittleness of pupils, sometimes flare up in a temporary loss of control.

The wish for security

I think an average person with average ability and good faith should be able to walk into most classrooms and teach. So I want a framework that allows me to do that. I don't think many of my colleagues do feel secure. I want security. I want action dealt with at the level my professional judgement says it's got to be.

(Teacher, Wilson, 2001)

Managing pupil behaviour was traditionally seen as one crucial aspect of the teacher's role, and teachers' reputations stood or fell on their skills as disciplinarians. In the past, to be known as 'hard' with difficult classes was a matter for professional pride, and to be regarded as weak was to mark one out as a failure. A teacher did not ask for help in managing a class unless he or she was admitting defeat. Classrooms were regarded as battlegrounds between the teacher and the pupils, and the teacher had to make sure he or she won the battle. Questions were not asked about how the teacher won, but it was tacitly understood that the fight was sometimes dirty: the chalk or the board rubber thrown across the room, the flat of the hand across the side of the head, the class bully pinned up against the wall and, at the milder end of the spectrum, the bellowing voice or the biting sarcasm, the petty belittling. Not all teachers resorted to such tactics, of course. There were those who could always rule benignly, through force of personality or the excitement of subject.

In 1987, physical punishment was outlawed and teachers were warned that any physical aggression against pupils could open them to prosecution for assault and battery. Long before this date, however, there was amongst many teachers and teacher trainers a groundswell of repugnance against the use of physical force and humiliating techniques to control classes. Strategies focused on psychological or sociological explanations for bad behaviour; the need for structure and consistent expectations; the building of good relationships with pupils. They emphasized the relevance of subject matter and the appropriateness of delivery. Many a young teacher came into their first teaching job full of idealism about how they were going to 'keep order', based on their respect for pupils, their firm expectations and their exciting teaching, and spent months of hell before it began to come right. For some it never came right, and they lapsed into traditional authoritarianism or struggled on as 'weak teachers' before succumbing to ill health and early retirement.

One of the problems facing teachers who did not want to be authoritarian, and that faced all teachers after the outlawing of any form of physical punishment after 1987, was the lack of consensus about alternative forms of classroom control. The predominant metaphor for classroom relationships was still that of a battle for control between the teacher and the dominant class members, but, in the eyes of some teachers, and the words of one, we were forced to face the battle 'with our hands tied behind our backs' (Wilson, 2001). A school I joined in 1987 had retained corporal punishment until legally forced to abandon it. There had been little discussion about the philosophical bases on which discipline should be founded or about the structures within the school to support discipline. Classroom management was considered the sole responsibility of the subject teacher in charge of the class and asking for help was a mark of failure. There was no consensus about school rules or expectations of classroom behaviour and few sanctions open to the teacher. There were no structured support systems. Apart from the long-standing and experienced staff, teachers and pupils alike were adrift in a sea of uncertainty and insecurity.

The statements of teachers at Eastbank School similarly revealed great insecurity about the standards of behaviour they were to expect from pupils and how to achieve these. A whole school discipline system had recently been introduced, but this was variously interpreted and implemented. In spite of an official ethos emphasizing teacher support and a no blame approach to difficulties in classroom management, one or two teachers reflected the traditional view that managing pupil behaviour was the teacher's individual responsibility, and to ask for support in this was a mark of incompetence.

Others were inhibited in asking for support because they feared that they would be perceived as failures. Some refrained from asking help from colleagues because they did not want to compound the disruption to their own lesson caused by pupils' recalcitrant behaviour, through having to disturb somebody else's lesson. There was provision for calling on senior management help in cases of extreme bad behaviour 'but no discussion about what behaviours are so unacceptable' (teacher, Wilson, 2001) to warrant the help. There were different perceptions about whose overall responsibility it was to work with teachers who were having particular difficulties with pupils, and doubts expressed as to whether there was anybody on the staff with the necessary sensitivity and counselling skills to undertake this role (a staff development tutor was later appointed – see Chapter 5):

> Before [the introduction of the discipline system] I thought I had quite high standards of what I wanted pupils to achieve and modes of behaviour in class, but obviously other teachers had different standards and different modes of behaviour . . .

> [prior to the introduction of the discipline system] Staff felt so isolated, because there was no set system or way of dealing with anything, so if they had to deal with something, if they took it on themselves, they had to take the whole thing on, and they would get lost and feel under pressure . . .

> Sometimes you need help, and know you will get the help and support you need, but fear that in asking for help you will be seen as a problem.
> (Teachers, Wilson, 2001)

There was ample evidence in teachers' statements to suggest that the overall perception by teachers in the school was that pupils' general behaviour in class was deteriorating and it was becoming harder and more stressful, even for experienced teachers, to maintain an orderly working classroom: 'The demands the kids make are far greater, much greater. The sorts of discipline we have to use are far greater. You can't just tell a child to sit down and be quiet' (teacher, Wilson, 2001).

Teachers therefore had an ambivalent attitude to support. On the one hand there was the tradition of individualism amongst teachers with a sense of pride in being able to handle difficult classes; on the other there was increased experience of isolation and the expressed need for support.

Feelings of isolation

Teachers' feelings of isolation were not just to do with feeling unsupported in managing pupils' behaviour. As one teacher expressed it, 'I feel like a little lost sheep' (Wilson, 2001). Several said that they never got any feedback from management about their performance as teachers. They did not know whether they were doing 'right or wrong', or whether their problems were common to other teachers as well as themselves. As one teacher said: 'It is also important that a teacher is told when she's doing OK otherwise she might sort one problem only to feel she has others' (Wilson, 2001).

In one or two teachers, the lack of positive feedback was experienced as a rejection of their particular skills and contribution to the profession, and therefore as a rejection of themselves and the kind of teacher they wanted to be. This had led to a certain amount of cynicism or alienation, and a self-marginalization of the individuals concerned: 'But then I do say again, I was far more appreciated by the senior staff in the previous school [that is, East-bank School before reorganization]' (Wilson, 2001).

There was evidence of communication gaps between management and staff, which led some teachers to experience a 'them and us' situation with management 'pulling in a different direction' and, in the perception of teachers, blaming the staff for a negative OFSTED report instead of 'us all having a cuddle and then working together' (teachers, Wilson, 2001).

It would be wrong to give the impression that Eastbank School was an unsupportive school. On the contrary, its structures were designed to be supportive to pupils and teachers, and several teachers I interviewed, as well as outsiders coming into the school (student teachers, teachers new to the school, external consultants), experienced the school staff as supportive of each other 'as far up as you want to go' (teacher, Wilson, 2001) as well as the pupils. At the level of formal structures, therefore, and at the level of informal relationships between colleagues, there was a lot of support. But at the deeper level of personal emotions, uncertainties and insecurities, many teachers felt unsupported in the kind of teacher they wanted to be.

So far, I have suggested from teachers' own statements that secondary school teachers accept a dual responsibility for communicating a subject and for pupils as individuals. The significant point is that both these responsi-bilities are to do with interaction and relationships. Many teachers are want-ing to be people sharing enthusiasms, knowledge and skills, understanding and values with young people rather than just playing the role of teachers teaching subjects to pupils. They want to be teachers as people interacting with pupils as people (*cf* Cronk, 1987). This is not so different a conception of teaching from that of primary school teachers, particularly since the intro-duction of more differentiated subject expertise in primary schools. They are vulnerable to frustration in both these professional aims and the overriding impression given, at this particular moment in Eastbank School's history, during a time of constant upheaval, OFSTED inspections, changing manage-ment personnel and styles, was that teachers were feeling generally stressed and demoralized, unsure of themselves and unsupported by the system.

In fulfilling this dual responsibility, teachers present themselves in certain ways. I look further at the metaphors teachers used in talking about their professional role, and distinguish between different orientations to their role or modes of presenting themselves. I suggest that these orientations reflect different ways in which teachers conceptualize the job of teaching and their professional values and purposes, and may stem from relatively stable and deep-seated aspects of teachers' personalities. Challenges to these arising from teachers' inability to be the teachers they want to be may cause great distress and demoralization.

Entertainers, gurus and mentors

I have used these terms to characterize groups of related metaphors used by teachers in talking about their work. These are not firm categories that may be used to label individual teachers, nor distinct teaching styles that may be adopted or changed as appropriate. They are expressions of the values and objectives that inform the individual teacher's work combined with the teacher's own personality and way of interacting with the world. However, they are not immutable and they may overlap in individual teachers. I shall briefly describe these with examples taken from teachers' own statements.

The teacher as entertainer

> These kids here, most of them don't want to learn anything, but some-times they love it so much that I'll do as much as I can for them, so they enjoy it . . . In a classroom now I can do what I want to do, for example give them a fun lesson, or do a skill, make it fun, and they will respond to it a lot easier. And I enjoy that, because I know that they're enjoying it and want to do it.
>
> (Student teacher, Wilson, 2001)

Teachers talk about providing opportunities for fun and enjoyment; of the 'buzz' of knowing you have carried a whole group with you to a new level of understanding. Performance imagery abounds. But the teacher as enter-tainer is an ambivalent image. Teachers may deliberately set out to enter-tain, or they may just as easily find themselves the object of fun or mockery. They use the imagery of circuses to denote both these aspects: the juggler who fails to keep the balls in the air, jumping through hoops, performing animals. They become the victims and scapegoats, 'rushing round like a headless chicken' and having to deal with disruptive pupils 'with our hands tied behind our backs'. This teacher identifies one of the drawbacks of the teacher as entertainer:

> Kids are bored in the classroom because they are so stimulated else-where. We have to compete against very professional people like [the makers of] television, video games, cinemas etcetera, and it causes no end of problems. We can't compete with televisions; we haven't got the skills or the technology to compete to entertain children, because that is

what we are told we have to do: we have to hold their attention so they will learn. We are professional teachers, we are not . . . well, I suppose we are partly actors, but how can we compete against television? How can we compete against video games which are one to one? I just think we are going to have to totally rethink, if we're going to do this.

(Teacher, Wilson, 2001)

The teacher as guru

'It's like the Greeks . . . I wanted to be Alexander's tutor, sitting in a fig grove, and people just sat at the foot of the master and . . . learning, because that's what it's all about. And that's how I saw myself when I was 12, 13. I wanted to be a teacher because I wanted to do it like that' (member of the support staff, Wilson, 2001).

The characterization of the teacher as successful entertainer conjures up the image of the teacher as solo artist enthralling an audience. When charismatic performance is combined with inspirational message, you have the teacher as guru. The teacher below quoted his pupils describing him as 'a mad scientist, walking on water', such was his devotion to his subject, which he had embraced and taught 'with all the enthusiasm of a convert':

> I think most of us would argue that education . . . has a value in itself; and it's something that I feel that, given a disciplined atmosphere, I could transmit to the majority of kids, and perhaps restore that wonderful atmosphere which you get into in a class, when the children really do place enormous faith in you, and enormous reliance on you, and believe everything you say . . . It's inebriating almost.

(Wilson, 2001)

An almost messianic stance characterizes these teachers and their belief in the importance of the knowledge they want to convey, and it is significant that the authors of these quotations had, in different ways, both distanced themselves from mainstream teaching to work on the periphery of the education system, because they found the realities of contemporary mainstream education incompatible with their own visions of what teaching should be about. Everyone remembers the one or two inspirational teachers in their own school days, and which of us has not dreamt of captivating 9D last lesson on Friday afternoon with the brilliance of our performance? Does the disillusion with their own dreams, which occasionally crept into the voices of some of the participants, signify the end of the teacher as charismatic performer and preacher? Is this a loss to our concept of teaching or is it no longer an appropriate image for today's teachers in a utilitarian world and in an educational ethos that stresses activity and participation and designates the teacher as a manager or facilitator of learning?

The teacher as mentor

> With my subject I find that I do have to give quite a lot of concentration. I want to know what the child is saying, what they're thinking, how they're doing something, and I find it difficult to keep an eye on the rest of the group in general. I tend to teach a lot of the time individually.

> [talking about the discipline system] I think there should be another step in the middle, before coming back into lessons [after a period in remove] . . . some chance to have a discussion with the child, and say, well this is why you ended up in this situation. Are you going to do something about it so that it doesn't happen again? . . . I do think there's something missing there between the teacher and the pupil.
>
> (Teachers, Wilson, 2001)

The flamboyant style of the charismatic teacher captivating an audience does not suit all teachers. Many prefer to work largely with individuals, using the pupil's perceptions as a starting point and helping them to work through difficulties – both intellectual and social or personal. Some teachers expressed a preference for this way of communicating a subject; and others specifically mentioned the satisfaction they derived from pastoral work with pupils. Whereas the entertainer and guru orientations imply a highly visible teacher persona affecting the emotions and thinking of a whole group of pupils, the mentor orientation requires a more reciprocal relationship with individual pupils.

Teaching – an emotional profession

The significance of all these orientations is that in some way they all imply interaction between the teacher and the learner. Even the apparently one-way communication of stage or pulpit involves a reciprocal feedback and influence. Have you ever been in a theatre where the atmosphere between actors and audience is electric with shared emotion and insight? Teaching is an essential human activity. Most adults try to influence the young in some way, or to share knowledge and insights with others because they want to share the excitement and importance of what they know. BBC *Newsnight* (12 February 2003) showed a voluntary group of young black people learning to play steel band music so that they could then share these skills with other young people. Asked how it felt to learn and pass on their knowledge to others, they testified to the excitement and increased feelings of confidence and self-worth they experienced.

People often talk as though emotions should be banned from the teaching relationship. Impossible. Emotions are at the heart of the teaching relationship. People see reflections of themselves in the way other people respond to them. This is nowhere more true than in the teacher–learner relationship.

If pupils seem to be enjoying the teacher's lesson and learning from it, the teacher feels good about him or herself and his or her commitment to teaching is reinforced. There is evidence from teachers' own statements that they were passionately committed when they began their teaching careers.

But emotions in teaching can be negative as well as positive, and negative emotions may have malign effects on teacher–pupil relationships. Teachers' commitment and the kind of teacher they want to be is based on deeply held personal and professional values. There is evidence that the disjunction teachers feel between the teacher-person they want to project and the kind of teacher they perceive themselves to be in their classroom practice and in the way others respond to them causes great distress and distorts their classroom relationships further. Teachers' statements testify to the anguish they feel when they find themselves behaving towards pupils in ways they condemn in themselves, and that are the antithesis of how they set out to behave. Part of that anguish resides in being perceived as someone you know you are not, as the teacher quoted on page 24 reveals, and as this teacher says: '[I need to] find the space to relax more and be myself, so I can be more confident and can help individuals in the way I want to . . . I'm sometimes afraid they think I don't have a sense of humour' (Wilson, 2001).

Much of teachers' current stress and demoralization is attributed to the rates of change in educational thinking and structures, their increased workload and the pressures on their time, and these undoubtedly play an important part at the level of political decision-making and educational policy. Lack of time is a universal cry amongst teachers. But to support teachers effectively, it is necessary to examine how these factors impinge on teachers' self-image, and on their ability to be the kinds of teachers they want to be. If teachers cannot feel good about themselves in the classroom, there is little chance of them being able to cause pupils to feel good about themselves. As Woods (1990, p 181) said: 'If a teacher is forced to be a police officer or drill-sergeant or welfare officer; or to be traditional when progressivism is the aim, or to shout at or be nasty to pupils on occasion when it is not in one's character to do so, what is it doing to the teacher as person?'

And what happens to teachers when their characteristic way of presenting themselves is frustrated? How does it feel when you have spent hours preparing stimulus materials to introduce a new topic, and the lesson is sabotaged by a handful of disrupters; or you embark on a lively presentation, and the class is clearly unresponsive; or you plan activities that allow you to work with individuals, but so many pupils require attention that you cannot get round to everyone before they become frustrated, bored and restless? I had successfully worked with home-made puppets to introduce topics in German to year eight groups. So during a school exchange to Germany I treated myself to a pair of beautifully made genuine German puppets and tried them out on my current year eight group who were a difficult class, and whom nothing so far had motivated. I was treated to hoots of derision and the accusation that I was treating them like babies. Having by this time exhausted all my strategies with them, and feeling particularly stressed at the time, I lost my temper with them out of sheer frustration and a major confrontation followed. A year later I was using the puppets with a group of the same age, and they asked for them over and over again.

On another occasion, with a different year eight group I had spent time inventing a revision and consolidation game to keep part of the class occupied while I worked with the rest of the class. Within a few minutes, the cards had been thrown all over the room, and I had to get the whole class simply copying lists of vocabulary to restore order.

The point about such incidents is that I continually experimented to find ways of motivating and involving pupils and so often had to resort to routine, unchallenging tasks, which the pupils, however, regarded as legitimate work. The sense of failure was two-fold: the fact that activities I had spent a lot of time planning did not work, and the fact that I was reduced to teaching in ways I despised. The accumulated frustration sometimes led to emotional explosions on my part at the disruptive activities of certain pupils and ruined my relationships with the group. I began to resent the teacher persona that I was projecting: inconsistent, boring, irritable, easily provoked; and a dangerous hiatus developed between this apparent self, and the personal and teaching ideals I had always had.

Implications for support

My own research and that of others in both secondary and primary teaching (Nias, 1989; Woods *et al*, 1997; Wilson, 2001) suggests that the ideal teacher image that individuals have of themselves reflects deeply held philosophical values about the nature and purposes of one's work, and that where these purposes are frustrated, serious stress and demoralization can arise. Yet, given the current climate and conditions under which teachers work, the range of pupil needs to be catered for, the multiplicity of curricular and assessment demands, the lack of consensus about the aims and purposes of education and the complexity of classroom relationships, it is not surprising that teachers sometimes fail to live up to their own standards, and frustration, guilt and stress ensue.

The teacher who relies on charismatic performance and inspirational leadership is in competition with sophisticated media and electronic entertainment and the values of footballers and pop idols, and may be at best ignored, at worst rejected. The teacher who relies on forging individual relationships and meeting individual needs is constantly challenged and frustrated by the sheer volume and pressure of those needs often aggressively expressed. To maintain control of themselves and the class, teachers need support, but it is not always clear what kinds of support are appropriate and acceptable, given the tradition for teachers to manage classes unaided.

Extrapolating from teachers' statements, I have identified the areas of teachers' current experience that potentially lead to frustration. All are characterized by teachers' sense of not being able to function properly as the teachers they wanted to be. Readers may judge for themselves the extent to which they identify with the experience of Eastbank teachers.

Barriers to fulfilment of purpose

Inappropriate curricular requirements

Several teachers expressed reservations about recent developments in secondary school curriculum and assessment requirements. They felt these were often inappropriate to their pupils' needs, and denied teachers the freedom to select and deliver curriculum projects in the ways they judged most suitable for their particular classes. They resented the detailed written planning that had to be undertaken and the diminished room for manoeuvre that these highly structured requirements allowed.

General increase in administrative responsibilities and paperwork

The effects of the increase in paperwork and the resultant 'intensification of teachers' work' (A Hargreaves, 1994; Woods *et al*, 1997) have been well documented in recent years and have had some recognition in the more recent statements emanating from the DfEE. But it is necessary to ask the question: in what ways does this paperwork detract from teachers' 'real work' (Gewirtz, 1996)? Do all teachers reject the need for all the paperwork that is now required of them? The paperwork includes: the detailed curricular planning referred to above; the recording and assessment of pupil progress and the attendant testing, marking and reporting; the preparation of individualized work, the drawing up of Independent Learning Programmes and the reporting on progress accompanying the legislation around special educational needs. Statements made by Eastbank teachers suggest that not all paperwork is seen as unnecessary. There is just too much of it and too little time in which to do it without seriously jeopardizing the quality of the work that goes on in the classroom.

Lack of time

Not having the time to do all the things that had to be done outside the classroom, nor having the time in the classroom to respond flexibly and appropriately to all the situations that might arise was clearly a cause of considerable frustration and increasing stress amongst the teachers who talked to me. The lack of time might arise from all the administrative work as outlined above, or it might arise from the overwhelming needs of individual pupils in the class. The two are connected. The administrative tasks allow teachers less time and opportunity to give pupils the attention they need, or to intervene quickly in classroom disturbances. Pupils needing attention become frustrated, bored and restless, creating escalating classroom management problems.

Lack of emotional space

Lessons that are constantly disturbed by restless or alienated pupils, where teachers do not have the time to deal with these disturbances appropriately to the situation and to the needs of the pupil and the rest of the class, become fraught with tension, antagonisms and conflict. Without teachers intending it to happen, confrontations arise that further sour relationships between teacher and pupils, creating a classroom ethos in which it becomes increasingly difficult for teachers to be and act the teachers they want to be. As I shall show later, both teachers and pupils lack the opportunities to distance themselves from conflictual situations, to allow emotions to subside and to create space for considered actions and reactions.

Lack of certainty

Eastbank teachers offered evidence of feelings of intense uncertainty and insecurity to do with their professional role, the standards of behaviour they should expect of pupils, ways of dealing with difficult classroom behaviour, the degree of support and back up they could expect from senior management for their actions, the lack of positive and constructive feedback from middle and senior management. They experienced considerable isolation, and lacked a secure framework of reference within which to site their own work and the contribution they made to the school.

Lack of a common structure of values and standards

Related to the above was the lack, experienced by many teachers, of a guiding set of principles that underpinned their work, together with a school-wide, consistent system of rules, rewards and sanctions to govern pupils' behaviour and teachers' reactions to it (prior to the introduction of a whole school discipline system). Inappropriate and disruptive behaviour from pupils prevented teachers from delivering lessons in the way they wanted to, interfered with other pupils' learning and contributed to stressful and conflictual rather than collaborative and harmonious classroom relationships. Much of the time, in dealing with disruptive behaviour, teachers felt very much on their own.

Lack of freedom for professional judgement

The other side of isolation is autonomy. What is experienced by one teacher as isolation in having to deal unsupported with a disruptive and destructive pupil may be welcomed as autonomy by teachers who choose to teach and manage classes in the way that they feel best suits themselves, their own personalities and the teaching situation they find themselves in. This tension between isolation and autonomy is a core dilemma in teachers' perceptions of their support needs.

Inadequate communication

I have several examples of communication gaps and partial perception between teachers and management. Teachers sometimes felt that management did not support them in their efforts to deal with behavioural problems. Before an OFSTED inspection, which staff were expecting to be highly critical, they felt that the finger of blame was already falling on them and were resentful. Through my own conversations with senior management staff, I gained a much more positive impression of the regard in which management held most of the staff and their awareness of how exhausted and demoralized staff were. Somehow these messages were not getting through, partly I suspect because of the defensiveness and anxiety that the OFSTED inspection and its aftermath were causing across the whole school.

Teachers' overriding need was to be allowed to do the job they came into the profession to do. They wanted to be able to teach the lessons they had spent much time and energy preparing, and they wanted to be able to do this with due attention to the individual needs of pupils. They wanted to remain calm and relaxed enough during lessons to project their real selves in the classroom and to respond constructively to pupils' behaviour. They wanted to continue to enjoy their teaching, to convey the excitement and importance of their subject and to stimulate in their pupils a similar excitement in learning. They wanted to feel that they were not working in a vacuum, that the standards they expected from pupils were shared and reinforced across the school, and that they could call on support when necessary without compromising their professionalism. They wanted validation of their own role, to be part of a team, to be consulted and kept informed, and to contribute to developments and improvements within the school. They needed recognition and appreciation of their efforts, and positive and constructive feedback.

Summary

Using the words of teachers from Eastbank School, I have described how they perceived their ideal professional role and how they experienced it in reality. I have identified some of the obstacles that prevented these teachers from being the teachers they wanted to be. These can now be translated into support needs. These are:

- a need for certainty concerning values, standards and expectations;
- a need for a sense of security and back up in dealing with difficult individuals and groups;
- a need for a sense of belonging and freedom from isolation;
- a need to contribute and feel valued;
- a need for positive and constructive feedback;
- a need for self-directed professional development opportunities;
- a need for the opportunity to teach according to one's own philosophy and values;
- a need for validation and confirmation of one's teacher identity and values and purposes;
- a need to retain one's humanity.

A number of support initiatives were in operation during the period of my fieldwork. I shall describe and discuss these in Chapter 3 in the light of the needs identified above. But the overarching need is for the conditions that allow teachers to carry out on society's behalf the essential function of teaching and socializing the young, and to be able to do this in a humanistic way as role models for a mature, proactive, continually learning and caring community.

2 From where I sit

Pupils' perceptions of their needs

In Chapter 1, I focused exclusively on teachers' perceptions of the job of teaching and the obstacles to performing the work according to their own ideals. But teaching is interactive work. Where there are teachers there are learners, and successful teaching and learning depends on the needs of both being met. A major theme of this book is that much classroom disruption occurs through a clash of needs and a clash of perceptions. Teachers cannot be effectively supported without taking into consideration pupils' needs and their perceptions of what is going on in the classroom. This chapter is therefore devoted to describing pupils' classroom needs based on informal and semi-structured interviews with pupils at Eastbank School, reinforced by conversations I have had over the years with pupils I have taught.

My personal professional diary records the following episode from my own teaching experience. I am talking to Kevin, a member of a mixed ability class which has a reputation throughout the school for difficult behaviour. Kevin causes me a lot of concern. At the beginning of the year he was polite, alert and responsive, and showed some aptitude for my subject, French. I am talking to him after yet another lesson when he has deliberately tried to wind me up with petty disturbances: silly noises, paper aeroplanes, general inattention. He does not look happy. This is what I wrote:

> Had a long talk with K who started the year in September as one of the most cooperative lads in the group and has become one of the most deliberately provoking. He confirmed D's [another boy in the group] earlier account of group pressures to go along with the 'hard' disruptive elements in the class. [K] said only A [girl] was able to stay completely out of the pressures and she was left alone. The rest daren't appear to work.
>
> (Wilson, 2001)

Many other such statements and remarks, and the incidents I witnessed, are testimony to the fear many pupils live under in classroom and playground if they appear to be too conforming to the teacher's expectations of behaviour. This fear is not restricted to the experience of what are perceived to be the weaker victims of the school or class bully, although I have witnessed plenty of that. It is not a fear simply of petty or severe violence directed against them. It is the fear, at an age when being one of the gang is so important to young people, of being thought odd, not one of us, ostracized. So, in a class group where the dominant ethos is rejecting of school in general or of particular subjects or teachers, you engage in very visible teacher baiting to earn your credentials with the group leaders. Most teachers have had to experience at some time the irritation, frustration and perhaps personal affront that this constant disruption and sometimes bitter confrontation causes, but while licking their own wounds may fail to perceive the very real conflict, even anguish that many normally decent young people feel when they are caught between conformity to teacher expectations and acceptance in the peer group.

Classroom management has traditionally been conceptualized as a battle for control between teacher and pupils. The attempt to win the battle and be seen as strong has sometimes blinded teachers to the complexities of the emotions and needs of the young people who seem hell bent on destroying lessons. Even the apparently hard-bitten may show the most touching vulnerability when caught off guard. One boy did everything he could to make life unpleasant for me, barracking me constantly during lessons, drawing obscene pictures on board and desk, hurling personal insults at me until 'one such remark actually alienated him from the rest of the class who dissociated themselves from it, leaving him exposed, embarrassed and blushing' (personal professional diary, Wilson, 2001). Here are some more examples from my diary:

> J, with whom I had had several brushes the previous year [during German lessons] found herself to her dismay placed in my tutor group. Determined to become one of the influential members of this new grouping, she ostentatiously walked out to the front of the class and wrote on the board: 'Class Ten X versus Mrs Wilson'. I said 'Why did you feel you had to do that, J?' and somebody else went out unasked and rubbed it off the board. So J tried again: 'Class Ten X versus teachers'. But nobody in the class responded, so J slunk back to her place and kept quiet for the rest of the session.

> M, a year ten boy who had tried in class throughout the year to systematically destroy me, thanked me one day for having been understanding during the previous lesson in allowing a friend to go out of the classroom with him to talk when he was in tears about a break up with his girlfriend. This did not alter his attitude to me in class . . . but it did give me a glimpse of a much softer lad than the hard bully he usually displayed, and hinted at the conflict going on in himself between his private and his public persona.

> (Wilson, 2001)

This last example is particularly significant, because like the anecdote at the beginning of the chapter, it points to a similar experience of disjunction between one's real self and the self one is projecting in public, as discussed in Chapter 1 in relation to teachers. The incident with the girl, J, is also revealing for the 'battle' language she uses: 'Class Ten X versus . . .', illustrating the perceptions that pupils also hold of the classroom as an arena of war, and teachers as the natural enemy.

So, on the one hand, pupils subscribe to the 'them and us' attitude to teachers, and have to make sure that they are seen to be 'one of us'. On the other hand, particularly as individuals, away from the group pressures, they respond to the teacher who acts with human sensitivity to their individual needs at a vulnerable time in their growing up. This paradoxical relationship creates a dilemma for teachers who have to gauge which scenario pupils are acting out at any given time.

Pupils' behaviour

The Elton Report (1989) confirmed what teachers had experienced for some time, that pupils' behaviour in schools was becoming harder to deal with, and subsequent reports and government statements suggest that the situation has not improved in recent years. There has been a swing in attitudes towards the causes of bad behaviour, from attributing blame to the child, the family and the social environment to blaming schools and teachers. I suggest that the factors contributing towards pupils' behaviour in class are complex and that unidimensional explanations are not helpful. To attribute bad behaviour solely to the child's personality or background is to ignore the contribution schools and teachers can make to children's development, and takes the responsibility away from individual teachers to scrutinize their own practices. Conversely, to apportion blame solely to the school and the teachers is unrealistic, and in cases where the school and the teachers are self-critical and willing to modify their behaviour, is likely to generate demoralization and resentment.

In Chapter 1, I suggested that many teachers are committed, imaginative and sensitive, working flat out to fulfil their dual responsibility to subject and to pupils, and yet find the management of some class groups and some individuals very difficult. I gave examples of the kinds of behaviours that confront teachers, ranging from the petty but insistent disruptions that destroy lessons and erode a teacher's energy, through outright defiance of the teacher to aggressive verbal and physical behaviour against the teacher. During my teaching career in comprehensive schools, I have been jostled, insulted, sworn at, spat at and had missiles thrown at me. Referring to my fieldwork period in Eastbank School I recorded:

> In classroom observation and through volunteering to work as a support
> teacher for some groups, I was able to watch how some pupils treated

some teachers, and to expose myself to pupils' attitudes and willingness or not to cooperate. In several classes that I observed, continuing talking to the point where this became overt defiance of a teacher's instruction was evident, and to an extent where it disrupted the delivery of the lesson, or took attention away from legitimate activities. There was indignant 'answering back' when teachers took action to correct a pupil's behaviour. I heard rude, occasionally foul comments directed 'sotto voce' against a teacher, and I heard a pupil openly swear at a teacher. I myself experienced pupils ignoring me and talking socially across me when I was working with them. I was told by a girl under her breath to shut up, when I asked her to stop her private conversation while I was trying to help her. I have been referred to as 'that old granny', had my appearance publicly and negatively commented on, been exposed to ribald comments and gestures, and told to fuck off.

(Wilson, 2001)

Undoubtedly, some pupils behave badly because they are acting out in the classroom or in the relationship with the teacher, a deep unhappiness that has its roots elsewhere. Others are provoked by tensions and interactions within the classroom, sometimes initiated in the peer group, sometimes arising from the teacher's attitudes and responses. As this teacher remarked: 'You found yourself going over the top over something very minor, and it used to affect the rest of the lesson, and obviously the quality of teaching in that lesson . . . If I'm shouting at them, it's quite natural for somebody to shout back at me' (Wilson, 2001).

But there are also pupils who do not come from socially or emotionally disadvantaged backgrounds, who do not have special educational needs and are able to cope with the work, but who appear to make a considered decision to behave badly based on their assessment of the likely consequences to themselves from the peer group if they conform to the teacher's expectations, and from the teacher and the institution if they don't. Measor and Woods (1984) describe from their detailed study of how children adapt to the transfer from primary to secondary school, the decision-making that appears to inform pupils' attitudes and behaviour in particular lessons: the perceived status of the subject, the perceived status of the teacher, the group dynamics, the teacher's personality and teaching styles.

My own diaries record these comments from pupils when talking about their own behaviour:

There have been fascinating indications emerging recently from the year eight group of collective attitudes to French. P said in reply from a comment from somebody that they didn't do much French at their primary school, 'Oh, we had a woman tried to teach us French for a year, but we soon got rid of her.' M, who had returned with F in the dinner hour to finish work, said, when asked why she hadn't worked hard to finish it, 'But it's French isn't it?' Me: 'What difference does that make?' M: 'But everybody mucks about in French in all schools. My friends in other schools make me laugh telling me what they do in French lessons.'

S and H doing detentions missed last week. Asked why they continue deliberately to misbehave in ways they are asked not to. 'To annoy you, Miss', says S. 'Everybody does it. It's fun', says H, 'It makes you look big with your friends.' 'You look soft if you just do as you're told and do the work', says S. 'It depends on the lesson', says H, 'German is just so boring.' This is a class who respond rather badly to 'communicative approaches' but will copy from the board and do exercises quite happily.

(Wilson, 2001)

In one school I was approaching the end of a two-term temporary contract. I was talking with a group who had been difficult from the start about their behaviour. They had had a number of short-term supply teachers, and had assumed I was just another. 'It would have been different, Miss, if we had thought you were permanent' (personal professional diary, Wilson, 2001).

Eastbank pupils' perceptions of their behaviour

The reasons for disruptive behaviour seem to be many and various. This section describes Eastbank pupils' attitudes to classroom behaviour as seen through their eyes. The material was collected during informal chat with individuals or semi-structured group interviews. I talked with 16 pupils in all. They knew why I was taking notes, or in the case of one group, tape-recording the conversation. The points I make here are distilled from these individual and group discussions. At the time the conversations took place, the school had been operating a whole school discipline system (see Appendix) for two years, involving a common set of classroom rules and structured arrangements for rewarding and sanctioning behaviour, therefore the pupils' comments have to be seen in this context. I first reproduce the findings as they emerged from the research and then comment on the implications with additional material from my own professional diaries. The discussions with the pupils were grouped around the following questions I set myself:

- How do pupils become aware of appropriate classroom behaviour?
- How do they perceive the rules?
- How are they made aware that they are behaving appropriately?
- What do they consider the best kind of reward for good behaviour?
- What happens if pupils are not behaving appropriately?
- What do they consider the best ways of helping them to behave better?

How do pupils become aware of appropriate classroom behaviour?

Several pupils mentioned that the rules were displayed in the classrooms, and that they had been explained to them and discussed with them at the beginning of the school year (as an introduction to the system for year seven and as a reminder for years eight and nine). Asked whether they were reminded of the rules at any other times, their perception is that the rules are reinforced when they are broken, either through tutors and class teachers talking to them, or by being made to write them out as a punishment. This perception of rules being learnt through being broken was expressed by different informants in different contexts. One informant indicated that writing out the rules is sometimes used as a time-filler at the ends of lessons for pupils who have finished their work. Almost all my informants were able to tell me the rules with very little prompting, although there were difficulties with one pupil who started at the school in the middle of the school year, and who had to pick up the system.

How do pupils perceive the rules?

Most of those I asked agreed both with having a system of rules and with the specific rules operating in Eastbank School. Without rules, they said, people would 'just do owt'. One or two individuals disagreed – not very seriously – with specific rules. Any reservations expressed were less to do with the rules themselves as with the way the system was sometimes implemented. They clearly perceived that teachers differ in the importance that they attach to particular rules and the action taken when rules are broken. This will be discussed in greater detail in the section on sanctions and in Part II.

How are pupils made aware that they are behaving appropriately?

However I varied the way in which I introduced the issue of rewards, it became clear that pupils were only hazily aware of having their appropriate behaviour acknowledged and reinforced, confusing rewards for general behaviour with those for good work or specific acts of helpfulness or service. Several pupils thought that the behaviour rewards were only for attendance in the lesson, although one ventured to suggest that they were also for homework and the presentation of work. Few informants were able to tell me of other ways in which they were made aware of behaving well. One said if you're behaving well, you don't get put in detention or remove. Another said if you're good and get on with your work, you don't get attention. (Does this mean: you don't draw attention to yourself?) One informant did say that you get 'pats on the back' from your head of house, and these were clearly appreciated if given discreetly, out of sight of friends. However, I received the impression that appropriate behaviour is recognized by pupils more in the absence of punishment rather than in the positive reinforcement of the behaviour.

Against the majority's somewhat neutral awareness of having their appropriate behaviour acknowledged, a small minority give a contrasting impression. They put great value on praise from teachers, tutors, heads of house and members of senior management as a way to make them aware that people are pleased with them and the efforts they are making to conform. They appreciate the fact that word gets round from teacher to teacher that they are trying to improve their behaviour. They mention teachers who make it clear to the class that the group's good behaviour gives them pleasure, and that they are personally saddened when a group gets itself into bother.

These contrasting impressions suggest to me that teachers may put great efforts into turning round individuals or groups who appear to be going astray, but for only too recognizable and understandable reasons are less consciously assiduous in reinforcing the appropriate behaviour of those who generally conform.

What do pupils consider the best kind of reward for good behaviour?

As mentioned above, one group was very clear that acknowledgement and praise from teachers was highly valued. Another group was unanimous in the value it placed on letters home to parents. Pupils like their parents being told that they are behaving well, although one informant mentioned that it was better to post the letters home rather than to embarrass them by handing them the letters in front of friends. It is noteworthy that pupils appeared to value these non-material marks of teachers' approval above the material prizes that resulted from the earning of a succession of certificates for good behaviour.

What happens if pupils are not behaving appropriately?

Most of my informants appeared to be fully aware of the system of sanctions, which consisted of an escalating range of punishments from a half-break detention, through full-break and evening detentions to a period in the 'remove room' excluded from normal classes and finally suspension or permanent exclusion from school. Pupils who have joined the school through the school year tend to have to pick up the system as they go along. On the whole they felt these consequences for bad behaviour were reasonable. Reservations concerned the ways in which they were sometimes imposed.

There was a feeling, at times strongly expressed, that teachers sometimes misinterpreted situations, misunderstood a pupil's motivations, did not always listen to a pupil's point of view. Mistaken assumptions of blame might be made; teachers might interpret uncertainty about the task to be done as unwillingness to do it. An initial misunderstanding on the teacher's part, said one pupil, sometimes led to an indignant reaction from the pupil, which then escalated, and got them into trouble for real.

Although some pupils felt that they did not get attention if they kept their heads down and got on with their work, others felt that teachers had no time particularly for individuals who were perceived as awkward or not very good at the work. On being asked whether there were ways of getting attention when they needed help that would not be considered disruptive, some mentioned that they should put their hands up, but that they sometimes had their hands up for a long time without response.

The perception that teachers sometimes do not have enough time for them was not always negatively expressed. There was an interesting recognition from more than one informant that teachers really do not have enough time to give each pupil the attention they need and check that all the class are working, or attend to all the things they have to do. Asked whether there was any opportunity to discuss with the class teacher incidents where they were thought to have transgressed, one group said that there never seemed to be a right time: there's 'always too much stuff going on', teachers have to give attention to the whole class, make sure everyone's working, attend to people coming into the class for some reason, consult with other teachers, tidy up ready for the next lesson.

Pupils were prepared to admit that they sometimes broke rules in full knowledge of the consequences. Examples included getting oneself into break detention to be with a friend, carrying on chatting in flagrant disregard of the teacher, reacting to lessons they found difficult with petty disruption. The majority were prepared to risk a break detention for this kind of resistance. There was a widespread feeling that break detentions are not regarded as serious; on the contrary some pupils were said to use them as ways of appearing 'clever' or 'hard', and instances were quoted of pupils who just treated detentions as 'a good laugh', although one or two admitted to feeling scared on the first, perhaps only time they had had a detention. Asked where they would be prepared to draw the line, several, but by no means all my informants, said they tried to avoid evening detentions: they didn't like walking home alone, parents might be cross with them, and they didn't like being shouted at by heads of house.

A minority were prepared to go all the way to remove (exclusion from normal classes and confinement to a special 'remove room' for a full day's lessons, or until the child's parent had contacted the school). There was a feeling, expressed by several informants, that remove was in some way preferable to being in lessons: you didn't have to do any work; the work was easier; or it was peaceful in remove so you could get on with your work. However, when pressed, most said, tellingly, that on the whole they preferred to be in lessons: there are too few people in remove, 'you can't do owt, just stick there doing your work and stuff'. Asked how their parents reacted to them being in remove, most of those who had spent time there said it depended on what they were in for. If it was seen to be something serious (defined by one pupil as 'having a load off at teachers'), parents would be cross; but if the reasons were not perceived as serious, or were felt to be the result of a teacher's misinterpretation of a situation, or personal dislike of a pupil, parents would shrug it off, or seek clarification from the school. Parents talking directly with the teacher involved was seen as helpful by pupils in clearing up misunderstandings.

Asked how far they would be willing to go in persisting in non-conformity, those pupils who were prepared to risk remove unanimously said that the threat of suspension would be the sticking point. In fact suspension was perceived by all informants as the deterrent, raising pertinent questions about why a few pupils persist into suspension. Clearly, the conflict between willed and involuntary behaviour is at work in pupils as well as in teachers.

What do pupils consider would help them to behave?

Asked what they felt would most help them to improve their behaviour, some felt strongly that they wanted teachers to attend more to their needs, to listen to them and to change the way they talked to pupils. There was a feeling that you might sometimes be labelled as a potential troublemaker if your brother or sister was. Some felt that separation from those who were habitually uncooperative would help them not to be drawn into trouble, or prevent them from being wrongly perceived as involved. Setting was mentioned as helpful in keeping those who did not want to work apart from those who did. One pupil thought teachers should still be allowed to administer corporal punishment. More teachers and other adults around the buildings and school grounds would, said one group, help to decrease things like truancy and litter.

Relationships rule OK, but rules are necessary too

The significance of the above findings lies in the following:

- pupils' appreciation of the need for rules governing behaviour;
- the association of their own appropriate behaviour with absence of punishment rather than with positive rewards;
- the importance that pupils attach to the interpersonal aspects of classroom management;
- the evidence that pupils also experience conflicting motivations in their classroom behaviour;
- the similarity between the needs of teachers and those of pupils in matters concerning effective classroom management.

The explicit display of school and classroom codes of behaviour is a controversial subject. Some teachers feel that the explicit display of rules for classroom behaviour should not be necessary at secondary school level. Some argue that rules should be discussed and agreed with the pupils themselves. Some want every detail of behaviour specified, others prefer to describe the broad principles that should govern specific behaviour. Some teachers feel that behaviour is not dependent on rules at all. My own teaching experience suggests that many children have only a hazy conception of what is appropriate classroom behaviour. To them, classroom behaviour is what the teacher allows, what they can get away with. They are motivated by the immediate consequences of their actions, not by any consistent principles of how one treats other people. The following is an extract from my personal professional diary: 'The lack of a consistent disciplinary framework left pupils confused. "Nobody ever tells us what the school rules are" and constantly trying to establish the limits: "What will happen if I refuse?" "What will happen if I don't come to detention?"'' (Wilson, 2001).

Eastbank pupils at least knew what the rules were, but their apparent linking of their own appropriate behaviour with absence of punishment is significant. It suggests that their knowledge of the rules belongs to a different level of operation than their actual behaviour. They will behave according to more immediate considerations, and if they do not incur sanctions then they must have been behaving according to the rules. They are still not regulating their own behaviour according to a consistent moral framework. The fact that they are uncertain about how their appropriate behaviour is rewarded also indicates that the way they behave in the classroom is only partly influenced by the structured behavioural system. There are clearly emotional reasons for their behaviour, which cannot always be controlled through reference to a rationally structured programme.

The importance pupils attached to the interpersonal aspects of classroom behaviour and the way it is managed by the teacher is highly significant. Not only do they attribute at least some of the reasons for their own bad behaviour to the ways in which they perceive teachers are treating them, but they also appear, from their own words, to respond best to efforts to help them improve their behaviour that are founded on positive relationships with the teacher and with other significant adults. In this context, it is not so much about how teachers are actually treating the pupil as how the pupil perceives the teacher to be treating her or him. In other words, pupils' bad behaviour may be the result of their misunderstanding of teachers' attitudes and motivations, just as teachers' behaviour towards pupils may also be the result of the teacher's misunderstanding of the pupils' attitudes and intentions. In Cronk's (1987) view much classroom conflict is the result of such misunderstandings, and in my diaries I describe situations in which such mutual misperception seems to be taking place: 'The children, too, are active in helping teachers to define and label the disruptive pupil. The more conforming pupils will encourage the less conforming ones to perpetrate the disruption, they will take advantage of the interruption caused and then resent being blamed alongside the habitually disruptive pupil' (Wilson, 2001).

I quote an incident concerning a usually cooperative girl who is ostentatiously swinging a pen by its tassel during my exposition of a language task. I ask her to stop. She does so without fuss, but a few minutes later hands the pen to another girl who is a habitual disrupter in the class. This girl, of course, starts swinging the pen even more blatantly, and when I confiscate it, grumbles loudly that she has ink all over her hands, and why can't she go and wash them. The first girl resents the fact that I have taken the pen, and can't understand why I also blame her for giving it to her friend in the first place. Quoting again from my diary: 'The class encouraged the scapegoating of certain pupils (by putting the blame on them for incidents of disruptive behaviour). When I tried hard not to "pick on" these pupils, this was bitterly resented by other pupils who were being sanctioned for similar but less frequent disruption' (Wilson, 2001).

What seems to be happening in the above situations is a clash of perceptions. The pupils, for their own reasons, are misinterpreting the motivations behind my actions, which I intend to be non-discriminatory and targeted at individual needs as I perceive them. Because I am unsure of their motivations, I may not be interpreting their perceptions and needs correctly and become frustrated and hurt by their apparent misunderstanding and rejection of my actions. This mutual misperception is likely to lead to confrontation.

Just as the emotional effects of misperception may result in classroom conflict, appropriate behaviour is also linked with the emotional effects of positive interaction with the teacher and other adults. From their own words, pupils are encouraged to behave well if teachers address them politely, listen to what they have to say, realize when they are not understanding the work and take the time to explain it; and when teachers reward good behaviour with verbal and non-verbal positive feedback. More adults around to give individual attention and guidance would help improve behaviour, they said. Contact between teachers and with parents to convey good reports or to iron out misunderstandings is also found helpful. A period in remove was positively welcomed by a number of pupils because it was a quiet atmosphere, a smaller group and they could get on with their work undisturbed with more adult help. In other words, pupils respond best in an atmosphere of positive human relationships, where they are treated with respect and given personal, individual attention.

At this point many teachers will switch off. 'But I do all these things', you will cry, 'Or at least I try to, and the little monsters still won't behave':

> A major cause of frustration and feelings of powerlessness was the fact that teaching methods and management strategies which were underpinned by person-centred, individualized approaches to teaching so

often appeared to be misinterpreted and rejected by pupils who were operating according to another agenda. Several entries in my diaries note that management strategies and teaching styles which theoretically should involve and motivate disaffected pupils in fact have the opposite effect: pupils appear to regard management strategies directed towards individual needs as indicative of weakness, and teaching styles designed to promote active participation as 'not proper work'. Their working perception of the good teacher appears to be one who 'makes' them behave, however persistently they resist, and who gives them conventional paper and pen tasks to do, in spite of finding these boring. Paradoxically, the more collaborative management styles, and more active learning tasks can produce excellent response from more able and generally cooperative pupils, with whom more directive and more formal styles also work.

(Wilson, 2001)

This observation raises the possibility that other factors are at work in motivating children to cooperate as well as the management and teaching styles of the teacher.

At the beginning of the chapter I gave examples taken from my own experience of pupils who showed evidence of being in a state of considerable conflict with regard to their classroom behaviour, both wanting and fearing to cooperate. Eastbank pupils also gave indications of the power of the peer group in regulating their behaviour. Looking hard, joining friends in detention or remove were cited as some of the reasons for bad behaviour. Physical separation from the more habitual disrupters, they said, would help them avoid being drawn into bad behaviour or being wrongly suspected of being involved.

Evidence for this deep emotional conflict is found even in the behaviour of the group leaders in a class:

In break detentions, youngsters like P, T and K [high status group in a difficult class] work really well and show a much more cooperative side of themselves, as though trying to show me that this is really what they are like. Then they can't sustain it during the lesson because they daren't lose their standing with their mates for being tough.

The year eight group were at their most cooperative and we had a most enjoyable lesson until about halfway through when they decided they were letting their 'bad' image down (one of them actually said this).

(Personal professional diary entries, Wilson, 2001)

The dilemma for the teacher is that pupils *want* teachers to be accessible, approachable and to treat them with respect as individuals; on the other hand they need teachers to direct, guide, at times even *compel* them to behave in certain ways. They expect teachers to take from them the choice of misbehaviour, to relieve them of the conflict going on in themselves between pleasing the teacher and pleasing their peers. Pupils expressed this dual attitude to me throughout my time back in secondary comprehensive schools. Towards the end of a two-term contract:

> Some of the most recalcitrant of my year nine pupils seemed genuinely sorry that I was leaving. During a project which involved one of these miscreant's love of football, he said, unexpectedly, 'I think you are quite a good teacher, Miss, if you could have controlled us better.' And others said things like, 'You should have made me work', 'You should make them behave, Miss', 'You were too soft, you should have been hard, you should have put the fear of God in us.'
>
> (Personal professional diary, Wilson, 2001)

Pupils' ambivalent attitudes were also evident in the other two schools I taught in:

> When my tutor group in School Two, with whom I had struggled, sometimes viciously, I thought, for two years, learnt that I was leaving the school, many, even boys, were tearful. I tried to comfort them by saying that they would get used to their new class tutor, just as they had got used to me. 'Oh no', said R, 'It will be different. You went on being nice to us, even when we were horrible to you.'
>
> (Personal professional diary, Wilson, 2001)

And in my School Three tutor group, I noted that one girl said, 'Miss, you would do anything for any of us, but you ought to be stricter' (Wilson, 2001).

So here is a double dilemma, for pupils and for teachers. If teachers treat pupils with respect as human beings out of their own (the teacher's) humanity, and try to be helpful, and to see a situation from the pupil's point of view, that puts pupils in a quandary. There is less overt justification for treating the teacher as an enemy to be vanquished, and yet their own standing with their peers depends on their bad behaviour, so they feel guilty. Pupils have to redouble their efforts to make teachers respond to their bad behaviour either by making themselves behave so badly that control of their behaviour is taken from them, and they can say, 'Well, I have to behave, I've got no choice.' Or they can make the teachers behave so badly, for instance through loss of self-control, that pupils can feel justified in regarding the teacher as an enemy, and fair game.

The problem for teachers, as Eastbank teachers pointed out, is that it is more difficult these days to make pupils behave by all the traditional strategies once employed, if those pupils are determined to resist. And on the whole, teachers do not want to be authoritarian, draconian and insensitive to the needs of children, which are often reflected in their bad behaviour. As one Eastbank teacher said, 'I see no reason why you should have to be tough or you should have to be strong or you should have to be indestructible or pachydermatous to survive in teaching' (Wilson, 2001). Teachers want to be able to be human beings.

But pupils sometimes give the impression that they want teachers to be draconian. I asked one group who had complained that I was not being hard enough what they meant:

> They found it difficult to define what they meant by 'hard'. When pressed, they admitted that they saw good teachers as authoritarian – imposing their will on classes; and they were extreme in their views of what punishments were appropriate to those who continued to disrupt: 'bawling out', sending to the head, corporal punishment. They seemed unable to appreciate the idea of graded sanctions. They expected teachers to reinforce their own scapegoating of the miscreants – blaming the disruption of the class on a few 'hard cases', not admitting that they all frequently made eager use of the disruption caused by their braver peers. There was much passing of the buck.
>
> (Personal professional diary, Wilson, 2001)

Yet, as has been seen, pupils also appreciate teachers who can behave like human beings, making allowances for pupils' moods and personal unhappiness, treating them as individuals with individual needs.

So what is needed to release both pupils and teachers from the horns of the dilemma they are both caught in, and which too often leads, indeed, to a bitter locking of horns? How can pupils and teachers be lifted out of this emotional paradox in which they appear to need different things while in fact wanting very similar things from classroom life? How can teachers give the necessary structure and guidance to behaviour, and ensure that appropriate behaviour happens, whilst also helping young people to develop their own self-control and their own accountability? How can 'hardness' and humanity be combined compatibly?

Supporting relationships

In Part I of this book, I have aimed to show how both teachers and pupils are often in a state of conflict between how they want to behave and how circumstances force them to behave. The emotional stress caused by this conflict may generate further misunderstandings and confrontations that lead to a downward spiral of spoiled relationships and alienation in both teacher and pupils.

Teacher support is therefore about creating an ethos in which benign relationships can flourish and in which teachers can provide the strong guidance about behaviour that pupils need while at the same time retaining their humanity and sensitivity. This implies that teachers themselves can feel secure in their expectations of pupils and confident of back up from the school hierarchy for the values and standards they try to uphold. This further implies that individual teachers' expectations reflect the common values that underpin the school as a community.

Teachers want classroom conditions in which they can remain human and be the teachers they want to be, able to communicate their subject in motivating and academically valid ways, and to attend to the individual needs of pupils. They need support that facilitates the performance of this dual role.

Pupils want teachers to be human beings, sensitive to their needs; disciplinarians, giving firm and secure guidance about their behaviour; and patient, inspirational teachers. Support is needed that allows teachers to be all of these things for pupils.

I have described teacher support as those attitudes, structures and provisions that enable teachers to be the teachers they want to be. It is possible to define different levels of support:

- *facilitative*: enabling teachers to function optimally;
- *preventative*: enabling teachers to avoid crises and confrontations;
- *restitutive*: enabling teachers to regain good teacher–pupil relationships, should critical incidents occur.

By looking at the needs and conflicts of both teachers and pupils, it can be seen that appropriate support structures may decrease the likelihood of failures in classroom management, but that misunderstandings leading sometimes to actual confrontation are inevitable, and may require support provisions external to the classroom to resolve them.

Specific support initiatives discussed in the following chapters include:

- a whole school behavioural system;
- extra adult support in the classroom;
- collaborative initiatives and peer support projects;
- the appointment of a staff development tutor;
- professional development opportunities.

However, I argue throughout that the most crucial aspect of support is an ethos that acknowledges the essential goodwill and humanitarian motivations of teachers and accepts that classroom management problems often arise through teachers and pupils presenting themselves in ways that cause themselves conflict, and through each misperceiving the motivations of the other. Support for classroom behaviour has to be seen as a whole school responsibility, not as that of the individual teacher working in isolation.

In Part II, I discuss several support initiatives, focusing on developments I researched in Eastbank School, backed up by my reading of the literature and personal experience of what is going on in other schools. In each case I examine the initiatives from the perspectives I have elucidated in Part I: the needs of teachers and of pupils.

Part II

Support – prop or validation?

3   A system with a human face

I think that the Assertive Discipline that was adapted certainly brought about a hell of a lot of peer support in that it's the one thing that brought the staff together, because it's a survival mechanism, isn't it, you know, this behaviour, which is really what we're talking about.

(Teacher, Wilson, 2001)

However I approached the topic of support with teachers, the discussion would lead eventually to the question of classroom management and pupils' behaviour. Where teachers chose to talk about the levels of stress they experienced because of changes in the curriculum and organization of learning, the talk was about the effect not just on themselves and on their personal lives, but also on the quality of their teaching and the reflection of this in pupils' attitudes and behaviour: 'The curriculum has changed very much indeed, and I think that because of that the quality of teaching is not as good as it was' (teacher, Wilson, 2001).

Where teachers feel that what is being demanded of them in terms of administrative paperwork takes time away from their direct interaction with pupils, and when they are not comfortable with the curriculum they are expected to deliver, they are being attacked in both aspects of their professional role: as subject teacher and as enabler of individual learning and development. They begin to feel that they are letting the pupils down.

Many teachers are quick to blame themselves when pupils begin to misbehave. They have been trained in an ethos of social and psychological awareness that encourages teachers to look at their own attitudes and values and at what they are actually doing in the classroom as important factors in pupils' resistance. They have become used to assuming that if they are presenting relevant material in ways that make it accessible to each individual, and if they are cultivating good relationships with pupils, then pupils will be willing to learn and classroom disruption is confined to a very few individuals with extreme behavioural difficulties. Like secondary school teachers all over the country, Eastbank teachers perceived a year on year deterioration in pupils' behaviour and many automatically blamed themselves: 'We have to deliver it [curriculum] according to schemes of work, and kids fail because they have no experience of it, they have nothing to base their work on . . . they find they're easily distracted . . . Because the kids fail, they misbehave, which interferes with other kids and it has a knock-on effect' (teacher, Wilson, 2001).

Several teachers talked about the constant hassle of managing pupils' behaviour and of keeping them on task. They talked of not being able to relax or be themselves in the classroom, and of responding in ways that were completely at odds with the kind of teacher they wanted to be: 'I do find that I'm having to be on my mettle. I'm not finding it easy to relax with any of my classes this year' (Wilson, 2001).

Many teachers will identify with the feeling of becoming distorted as a person. Classroom discipline is not just a technical problem of applying certain skills. It affects the interactional patterns within the class and ultimately the deeper relationships between teacher and pupils. Where these become distorted, the stress suffered by both teachers and pupils may become intolerable. Eastbank teachers identified classroom relationships as a key arena where they needed support.

As already discussed, schools and teachers tend to be blamed for pupils' bad behaviour. Prior to the 1960s, bad behaviour was explained by reference to pupils' individual personalities and character traits or their 'feckless families'. During the 60s and 70s, research indicated the extent of the influence of social class on pupils' attitudes to school and highlighted the culture clash between the middle-class-orientated education system and working class values. Other research into classroom processes showed how teachers' differential expectations could disadvantage those children from the lower social classes and from certain ethnic minority groups.

Rutter *et al*'s work, *Fifteen Thousand Hours* (1979), suggested that schools could in fact make a significant difference to children's progress and life chances by the way they are structured and organized and by the behaviour of the teachers. So teachers are now encouraged through their training to believe that if they are well prepared with appropriate, stimulating and well-structured lessons, and if their expectations of pupils' behaviour and achievement remain consistently high, and their relationships with pupils are good, there should not be significant behaviour problems. However, when committed teachers try to put into practice the principles in which they have been trained and in which they believe, and they are confronted with a more complex and challenging reality, they begin to lose confidence, to feel a sense of failure, and if they remain unsupported, to risk stress, loss of morale and ultimately burnout. There is nothing wrong with the principles, but teachers' individual efforts must be backed up by the organizational structures.

As I have demonstrated in Part I, classroom interactions are not wholly amenable to rational regulation. The emotional responses of both teacher and pupils also determine the course of the interaction, and these must be taken into account and built into the organizational support structures.

The Elton Report, *Discipline in Schools*, published in 1989, recommended the introduction into schools of structured, whole school discipline systems. Eastbank School introduced a modified version of 'Lee Canter's Assertive Discipline' (Canter and Canter, 1992) at the request of the teachers as its response to the perceived deterioration in pupils' behaviour. As structured whole school discipline systems have gained such prominence in recent years I shall organize the rest of this chapter around these, using Eastbank School's experience as an illustrative example. Details of Eastbank School's Assertive Discipline System (ADS) are given in the Appendix.

A whole school discipline system

Recommendations for whole school discipline systems grew during the 1980s and 1990s. They arose out of growing concerns about deteriorating pupil behaviour and the increasing research interest into teacher stress and the contribution to this made by teachers' difficulties in managing classrooms and their acute sense of isolation and sense of failure. They also reflected a concern about the inconsistent approaches to behavioural standards that pupils encountered as they moved from class to class around the school, leading to confusion about behavioural expectations and creating opportunities for manipulating teachers. Moreover, whole school approaches to discipline presented a positive alternative to corporal punishment, which was finally outlawed in 1987.

As a prelude to describing Eastbank School's whole school discipline system, I shall summarize some of the literature on whole school initiatives, focusing on what have been found to be their advantages and drawbacks.

Whole school approaches to classroom behaviour

> If there is a criticism to be made of classroom management research it is that it was rarely set within a whole-school context. It is our view that the efficacy of initiatives at this level is reduced if the environment into which they are introduced is not a sympathetic one. We believe that the impact that teachers make at the classroom level is significantly determined by the organization and ethos of the school as an institution.
>
> (Galvin and Costa in Gray, Millar and Noakes, 1994, pp 146–47)

Whole school behavioural policies seek to make explicit for both teachers and pupils what the parameters of acceptable behaviour are. They are partly a response to uncertainties and differences in perception regarding the values that underpin the life of the school and what are considered appropriate ways of conducting oneself. They also seek to provide consistency in the ways teachers across the institution encourage appropriate behaviour and deal with inappropriate behaviour. The rationale is that pupils need this certainty of expectations, reinforcement of good behaviour and the predictability of the consequences of bad behaviour in order to regulate their conduct and develop their own self-control. Many structured approaches to a whole school discipline policy emphasize the role of teachers' positive attitudes to pupils and positive reinforcement of appropriate behaviour.

A reading of the relevant literature (Gillborn, Nixon and Ruddock, 1993; Gray, Millar and Noakes, 1994; Blandford, 1998) suggests that the following factors are important in determining the acceptability to teachers of a whole school behavioural policy and its effectiveness as a means of supporting both teachers and pupils:

- the involvement of all the staff in discussion and identification of problems to do with behaviour management and their support needs;
- the involvement of all staff in identifying the underlying values that underpin the operation of the school and the way in which people treat each other;
- extensive discussion with parents, the community and the pupils about the values and behavioural expectations of the school;
- involvement of the whole staff in drawing up the ground rules of behaviour and in determining the ways in which appropriate behaviour is encouraged and inappropriate behaviour dealt with;
- structures at school level to support teachers' management strategies at classroom level;
- recognition that some confrontations with pupils are inevitable, and that teachers may need support in handling them; the ending of the isolation of teachers and the recognition that the behaviour of pupils is an institutional responsibility and not simply that of the individual class teacher;
- the encouragement of discussion about difficulties; the high visibility and availability of senior staff to promote trust amongst teachers and the confidence to admit to difficulties;
- consistency across the school in expectations of behaviour, and in teachers' ways of dealing with behaviour, compatible with the flexibility associated with different teaching contexts;
- time and opportunity to discuss different perceptions of a situation and to negotiate acceptable solutions;
- support mechanisms for teachers to call on when necessary in dealing with individuals;
- good communication between staff and management;
- opportunities for peer support;
- relevant in-service training and professional development opportunities.

In practice, the adoption and operation of a whole school approach to behaviour raises a number of potentially controversial issues, which need to be resolved. These include:

- the possible imposition on some teachers of ways of working and dealing with classroom situations, which run counter to their own teaching and management styles;
- the adoption of a theoretical approach to behaviour management that offends the principles of some teachers;
- the reduction of ways of relating to one another to the mechanistic application of rules, rewards and sanctions;
- the neglect of strategies based on relationships, discussion, understanding of pupils' perceptions and negotiation;
- an overemphasis on the rational bases of behaviour to the neglect of the emotional.

As my conversations with Eastbank teachers showed, the sense of being actively and collectively involved in developing school initiatives appears to be very important for teachers. The danger with whole school discipline systems that are devised elsewhere and imported wholesale into a school is that they become just another structure imposed on teachers from outside, whether or not they suit the ethos of the school and the teachers' professional values and preferred ways of dealing with things. Andy Hargreaves (1994) pointed out that the activity of teaching and all that that entails is to a great extent an individualistic and creative activity, which is not amenable to too tight an imposed structure. Somehow, the security and collective authority of a school-wide discipline system needs to be married to the need for creative autonomy and individual flexibility in implementing it. As I shall show, Eastbank School did not fully resolve the dichotomy implicit in these two needs.

For additional examples of approaches to whole school behavioural policies, I recommend the books quoted earlier (Gillborn, Nixon and Ruddock, 1993; Gray, Millar and Noakes, 1994; Blandford, 1998).

Lee Canter's Assertive Discipline

Eastbank School based their approach on Lee Canter's Assertive Discipline (Canter and Canter, 1992). As this particular system has been adopted by many schools, not without controversy, I shall spend some time in discussing this as a prelude to examining Eastbank School's adaptation of it as a case study.

Lee Canter's Assertive Discipline arouses strong reactions from teachers and educationists, both positive and negative. The restricted accessibility of the materials (obtainable mainly through recognized Assertive Discipline trainers), and the evangelical and exclusive manner of its promotion tend to be alienating. And yet, on reading the book, it is easy to see why it has an immediate appeal for some teachers. It takes seriously the very real problems that teachers face in managing classrooms, avoiding any hint of blame, and argues explicitly against 'the myth of the good teacher', which states that a good teacher should be able to handle all behaviour problems on his or her own and within the confines of the classroom. It recognizes the guilt that teachers experience when they fail to match up to the myth. It denies that appropriate curricula and teaching methods will in themselves, alone, produce cooperative behaviour from pupils. It talks about 'empowering' teachers to assume both the rights and responsibilities of creating a positive learning ethos and to assert the authority that the current social climate denies them. In other words, it is explicitly pro-teacher.

However, this pro-teacher stance does not prevent the approach from being also pro-pupil. It talks about the need for positive relationships between teacher and pupils, for measures that enhance pupils' positive self-image and sense of worth, for flexibility in determining for each individual when to invoke the negative consequences, and for special arrangements for pupils whose difficulties do not respond to the behavioural system operated for the class as a whole.

The main focus is on the relationship between each individual teacher and his or her class. Each teacher sets the class ground rules, ideally in discussion with the pupils, and determines the system of rewards and consequences (for infringements). The system for each class is endorsed by the head teacher, thus giving it institutional authority. Importantly, the system of escalating consequences for infringement of the ground rules includes referral to the head teacher, and, if necessary, instant removal from the classroom. In this way, the responsibility and authority of the individual teacher is encouraged, but given institutional support. It is in later developments of the system, in keeping with the increasing emphasis on whole school discipline policies, that some schools have introduced Assertive Discipline on a school-wide basis, with a common system of rules, rewards and consequences. The implications of this will be discussed when Eastbank School's adaptation of the system is examined.

The psychological underpinning of Assertive Discipline is overtly behaviourist. Assertive Discipline operates on the Skinnerian stimulus-response model, according to which pupils will be motivated to behave appropriately in expectation of rewards, and discouraged from inappropriate behaviour through the fear of punishment in the form of sanctions, although these are verbally disguised as 'consequences'. Canter emphasizes that pupils have 'choice' in their behaviour: they can choose to act in ways acceptable to the teacher and the classroom situation, and therefore be rewarded for appropriate behaviour, or they can choose not to behave appropriately, and risk the consequences.

For Canter, the key to encouraging good behaviour is consistency in the application of the system. He stresses the need for predictability, enshrined in the consistent systems of rules, rewards and consequences within a positive and caring classroom ethos. His main focus is on the interactions between the teacher and the individual pupil: how the teacher responds to the pupil's behaviour. I find missing from the analysis of pupils' motivation a realization of the complexity of the competing pressures on pupils and of their often incompatible and conflicting needs, which may sabotage any approaches to behaviour management based on a *single* model of human motivation and social learning.

Eastbank School's decision to use the Assertive Discipline System (ADS)

The decision to institute a whole school discipline system originated from the staff rather than from management. Following the publication of the Elton Report in 1989, the staff of Eastbank School undertook a project that looked at what went on in classrooms right across the school. In 1993, the school had an OFSTED inspection, which suggested that discipline around the school could be tightened up. As a result they decided 'that certain types of behaviour could be corrected, or made less of a problem, if we acted in certain ways, and really we wanted to start acting as a staff of sixty-four as opposed to sixty-four individuals' (teacher, Wilson, 2001). Although the major incidents of gross loss of control by pupils happened only rarely, there was much petty disruption taking place, which they felt could be altered by teachers changing their own behaviour.

Two members of middle management had the opportunity to visit a school that had instituted Lee Canter's Assertive Discipline with apparent success, and, crucially, found the teachers of that school very enthusiastic about it in terms of improved pupil behaviour. The two teachers from Eastbank School then set up discussions with staff and management about the feasibility of introducing the system into the school. Teachers agreed by a large majority to adapt the system for use in Eastbank School and management funded the purchase of the necessary training materials. A steering committee was set up to oversee the development of the system, and working parties involving a majority of the staff were formed to adapt different aspects of Canter's model to meet the needs of the school. At various points during the process, the teaching body, non-teaching staff, management, governors and parents were consulted. When the system was finally introduced, it commanded wide support. The process of adapting and introducing the system through staff participation and consultation was one of the most important factors in its widespread acceptance:

> So when this ADS was first suggested, if anything, for the first time that I can remember, it brought staff together so that we thought we were actually forming a policy, not that had been dictated by anyone higher up in the school, or by the local authority or by the government. All of a sudden we were doing it for our school and we were doing it together.
>
> (Teacher, Wilson, 2001)

The operation of the ADS

The teacher quoted below compares management handling of similar incidents before and since the introduction of the ADS. In the first quotation she is talking in interview about an incident that had recently happened, and how it had been dealt with through the ADS. Three coins were thrown at her as she was writing on the board, the third of which hit her. I ask whether she had felt supported in the action that was taken subsequently. She replied (Wilson, 2001):

> . . . I think it's about . . . we moan quite a lot about the senior management and what's backed up but that was one incident where I felt that it was considered to be extremely serious and there was a determination to find out who the culprit was, even though the circumstances are quite difficult to find out because they're like clams, they don't let on. The person we suspect did it, the other two members of the senior management also suspect it was this person, and it is just a case of waiting to see if we can catch this person out; but that pupil as well is being monitored throughout the school now. . . because things are coming to light about his behaviour, not just in lessons, but to and fro from lessons and about the school site.

I ask how the handling of the present incident differed from what she might have been able to do with a similar incident prior to the ADS (Wilson, 2001):

> I think the fact that I was able to leave the room, sort of briefly been able to discuss it with my head of faculty, I think normally [that is, previously] my head of faculty would have had to come up, would have had to deal with it in that situation . . . which would have meant another class being disrupted . . . that there was somebody available who has, I suppose, enough kudos within the school management structure to go away and deal with that has been a plus . . . I think. It would have been difficult to have got hold of someone . . . I would have ended up having to phone round every single deputy head's office just to find one that was free at that particular time. Having someone on call has made that easier. And it was fairly prompt . . . within five minutes.

In informal discussion following this interview the participant revealed that there were occasions prior to the introduction of the ADS when she had felt less supported. She quoted a particular incident when she had sustained a slight injury through breaking up a fight between two pupils in her classroom only to see them returned to lessons on the same day having 'made it up'. She had felt personally 'devalued'.

As I have mentioned above, Lee Canter's original model focused on the relationship between individual class teacher and the class. The teacher devised her or his structure for the class, which was agreed with the head teacher, thus ensuring institutional authority. Further institutional support for the teacher was assured by incorporating removal from the classroom to the head teacher's room as the ultimate sanction for pupils who failed to respond to the teacher's own system of consequences. Eastbank School changed the focus of the system in a number of significant respects.

A detailed outline of Eastbank's Assertive Discipline System is included in the Appendix. To summarize its main provisions: it comprised a whole school structure of classroom rules and arrangements for rewarding appropriate behaviour and sanctioning infringements of the rules; its success rested on the principle of consistency: that the same standards of behaviour should be encouraged in every classroom and that teachers should practise the same means of rewarding and sanctioning behaviour. Teachers were supported by five crucial provisions:

- a common system of rules, rewards and sanctions;
- collaborative working and collective decision-making;
- the setting up of a centralized detention system, staffed by teachers on a rota basis;
- a remove facility with instant access;
- an on-call rota of senior staff.

I will talk about each in turn, from the perspective of the support these afforded to teachers.

A common system of rules, rewards and sanctions

Prior to the introduction of the ADS, teachers felt themselves uncertain and isolated with respect to the standards of behaviour they expected from pupils and in the methods of encouraging this behaviour they adopted. They did not know how their individual standards matched up to those expected by other teachers and sometimes felt that their own high standards were being undermined by colleagues with lower expectations of pupils. Pupils, it was felt, were being subjected to different experiences of discipline, which depended very much on the personality of the individual teacher. The whole sphere of values and standards of behaviour was reduced to the specific interactions between individual teacher and the class, a context-specific interpretation of ethics: I behave in such a way because you make me; I have no personal responsibility for my behaviour. 'I think the main benefit is that staff now know there is a consistent policy, that what they say in the classroom, children can no longer turn round and say, "Oh well, Mrs So and So lets us do this", or "Mr So and So never shouts when we do it", that sort of thing. So now the children do know exactly where they are . . .' (teacher, Wilson, 2001).

The process of constructing a common system of rules for classroom behaviour and a school-wide structure of rewards and sanctions, which had the assent of the vast majority of the staff and was later approved by governors and parents, created a framework of values for the school that commanded widespread support and reflected the authority of the collective will. Individual teachers were no longer expected to fall back on the authority of their own personality, or failing that, abdicate authority to another, more senior or 'stronger' individual. Pupils could no longer regard the expectations of individual teachers as mere whims to be disregarded if they could get away with it. Teachers' expectations in terms of classroom behaviour were the reflection of the collective values and standards that formed the tangible ethos of the school and had the authority of the institution behind them. Pupils who continued to flout that authority would in the last resort come up against the full weight of the institution.

Teachers reported that the operation of a common system removed from them much of the hassle involved in managing pupils' behaviour and allowed the class to work more efficiently:

> I mean, sometimes you could jolly them along and it would all resolve itself; at other times you found yourself entering into a kind of confrontational situation; but the ADS to a certain extent removes all that, because they now know that if they don't do what they are asked to do, that something else will happen to you, and the teacher's just going to carry on teaching the rest of the group, and they are just going to accumulate more and more, sort of, penalties . . . I certainly don't raise my voice anywhere near as often as I used to; I don't get into confrontations anywhere near as often as I used to.
>
> (Teacher, Wilson, 2001)

Collaborative working and collective decision-making

The process of modifying and implementing the ADS was in itself supportive for teachers: 'In many ways, then, it has been our work, setting it up. I feel that reflects in the way members of staff use it' (teacher, Wilson, 2001). Many spoke highly of the spirit of teamwork that was engendered at this time and that continued well into the second year of the system. Staff stayed on voluntarily after school to contribute to meetings and working parties. Teachers told of colleagues who gave voluntary time to supervising the detentions once the ADS was up and running. There was a feeling expressed of 'all being in this together', of making school policy, instead of having it 'dictated from the top'.

Teachers who expressed reservations to me about the ADS nevertheless tried to operate it if they could in accordance with the agreed procedures, and were conscious of letting colleagues down if they were not following the system. The sense of working together with colleagues for the good of the school as a whole appears again in connection with another initiative undertaken in the school (see Chapter 5) and seems to be very important for teachers' motivation. Senior management teams do not always appreciate how important this sense of collegiality and collective influence is for teachers.

Anecdotal evidence collected at the time of my fieldwork suggests that schools that have tried to introduce versions of Canter's Assertive Discipline as a top-down directive without the long process of involving teachers in the discussions and decision-making, may face much resistance and rejection on the part of teachers. I suspect that the involvement of teachers in collaborative work with colleagues in faculties and across the school is an important ingredient of teacher support through allowing teachers to feel less isolated and giving them significance within the school beyond their subject and class teacher roles. I return to this theme later.

A centralized detention system

Prior to the introduction of the ADS, teachers were responsible for organizing their own detentions at break or lunch time. This meant that the teacher lost valuable relaxation or preparation time not only for the period of the arranged detention, but in following up pupils who failed to attend:

> [The ADS] makes life very simple in some respects. The children have some specific rules, and they know that if they transgress, certain things will happen. Before that was introduced, if you wanted to give people a detention you might say that you wanted six of them to come and see you at break and maybe two would turn up. And then the next day you'd try and catch up, and it could take you all week to get six children through a break detention, which meant that in the end they were winning because they'd lost one break and I'd lost five.
>
> (Teacher, Wilson, 2001)

The centralized detention system was supervised on a rota basis. The computerized recording system ensured that absentees from the detention could be followed up by middle management rather than by the class teacher who had issued the detention. The system was so welcome that in the first year of its implementation, teachers volunteered to help supervise over and above their allocated rota duty, so anxious were they that the system should be seen to work.

After the change of school leadership and the virtual dismantling of the ADS, responsibility for detentions reverted to the individual class teacher. Pressures on staff were by this time so acute that teachers avoided the time and effort involved in detentions by simply not giving them, without any evidence that pupils' inappropriate behaviour was being dealt with in any other way: 'So much time and effort is spent on following up pupils and incidents that it sometimes doesn't get done. People stop giving detentions' (teacher, Wilson, 2001).

There were anxieties attached to the use of the detention system as an integral part of the ADS. Teachers became aware that some pupils saw detentions, particularly at break time, as a way of proving to the world that they were 'hard'. They risked misbehaviour during lessons as a way of having a bit of fun or avoiding work they were finding boring or too difficult because break time detentions were not too serious, and they could advertise their street credibility through them. Some pupils deliberately misbehaved in order to join friends in detention.

The second major concern involved the rising numbers of pupils with special educational needs who were appearing in the detentions. Teachers were becoming increasingly aware that many pupils were simply unable to cope with the curriculum, and the frustration and boredom this was causing them resulted in detentions; or they were being sanctioned through sheer misunderstanding on the teacher's part as to why the pupil was not working.

Clearly, teachers needed a wider range of options for distinguishing and dealing with pupils who were genuinely in difficulties and those who deliberately set out to disrupt the lesson for their own purposes. As I shall suggest later, teachers need a classroom ethos that allows them the time and emotional space to make informed and considered decisions about individual pupils.

The instant access remove system

Prior to the introduction of the ADS there had been a mechanism for removing pupils from lessons for fixed periods of time for instances of extreme bad behaviour. This arrangement, however, did not allow teachers instant access to this facility. An application to place a pupil in the remove room had to go through official procedures, so it might be a day or two before it could be implemented. Faculties operated their own informal arrangements, whereby pupils might be placed outside the classroom door for the duration of the lesson, or sent to the head of department or faculty, or placed with willing colleagues. These arrangements were often inhibiting for teachers who did not want to involve colleagues or advertise the fact that they had management problems, and there was also the risk that pupils would continue to disrupt out in the corridor or in other people's lessons. For these reasons, the provision of an instant access remove facility, which was part of the official school-wide sanctions system and therefore had institutional authority, was greatly welcomed by teachers: 'The system worked because there was somewhere to send her . . . she had to be got out of the situation, so it worked . . . the system backed me up' (teacher, Wilson, 2001).

However, there were also anxieties attached to the instant access remove facility. Pupils could be sent to the remove room through two routes: firstly, if, within the space of a single lesson, they escalated up the sanctions system through the points system operating in the ADS, incurring a half-break detention, a full-break detention, an evening detention and finally a day in remove; secondly, in extreme circumstances, if they committed an act of severe disruption, aggression or disrespect they might be sent to remove without having first escalated up the sanctions scale.

Some teachers feared that the sanctions system was being invoked too quickly, or that teachers were interpreting the system too inflexibly without also attempting other means of deflecting bad behaviour or defusing a tense situation. Some pupils, they felt, were ending up in remove too easily and too frequently. And again, there was concern that many of these habitual visitors to the remove room were those same pupils who had special educational needs:

> I do try and use common sense with it, because within 10 minutes, sometimes, you could have four crosses on the board. The minute you open your mouth somebody will say something, or you see somebody chewing . . . I think other staff will vary in opinion because I think some staff . . . some pupils have only got to breathe and its [indicates writing name on the board] and they're off [on the sanctions scale leading to remove] . . . and I don't know whether that is the right thing with some pupils.
>
> (Teacher, Wilson, 2001)

Another teacher said: 'There's more and more [special needs] children ending up in remove' (Wilson, 2001). There was also concern about the quality of the work that was organized for pupils to do while in remove. Each faculty had to provide a folder of work that could be given to pupils in remove, but the tasks set had to be of a kind that needed little explanation or supervision by the teachers on duty in the remove room, and so tended to be undemanding time-fillers.

Clearly, teachers felt a need for instant access to a remove facility in order to relieve the tension of a particular episode and to allow the teacher to continue to teach the lesson, but also time and opportunity for follow up work with the pupil to be undertaken. Several participants regretted that the system did not allow them to liaise with the pupils before their return to normal lessons:

> I get children coming back into my lessons after having been in remove. I've had no contact with them . . . I think there should be another step in the middle . . . before they come back into lessons, some chance to have a discussion with the child, and say, well, this is why you ended up in this situation. Are you going to do something about it so that it doesn't happen again? I do feel that there's something missing there between the teacher and the pupil.
>
> (Teacher, Wilson, 2001)

But as with so much in the way teachers want to operate, time is often not available for the follow up work that teachers want to do: 'In an ideal world you'd take them through what they did and what they should have done . . . but to be honest it's rare for that to happen. You have to be realistic. I mean, it's time . . . Five minutes to see them, you've got to be free, you've got to find the pupil, and it creates tremendous problems' (teacher, Wilson, 2001).

The rota of on-call senior staff

> Since we've had the ADS I don't think I've had one [confrontation] at all, simply because if it gets to a serious stage, you just make a phone call and somebody else comes and deals with it, and that is what the pupils expect, they don't expect you to be on your own any more.
> (Teacher, Wilson, 2001)

At Eastbank, teachers had expressed considerable feelings of isolation, both in relation to the standards of behaviour they expected from pupils and in dealing with those pupils who rejected the standards and the teacher's attempts to persuade them to conform. They were still conscious of the tradition that expected teachers to be able to keep control of a class unaided and feared to be seen as failing in this if they asked for help. Pupils took advantage of teachers' isolation, playing one teacher off against another, pushing increasingly hard against the discipline of the lone teacher until incidents escalated into major events. Pupils also perceived the discipline of the teacher as an individual matter, and teachers' failure to control them as individual weakness. Teachers found themselves acting against their own nature in their attempts to control classrooms – a tension that itself distorted their responses and escalated situations.

There was a need, therefore, to provide back up for teachers on those occasions, when individual pupils or groups became seriously out of control, and refused to respond to all the other measures that the teacher had attempted. This back up needed to be available within an ethos that recognized a collective responsibility for discipline and a common set of standards within which the individual teacher operated. In this context, the senior member of staff was there to reinforce the authority of the teacher. The teacher's authority was no longer to be regarded as individual idiosyncrasy but the reflection of a collective system of values and standards, which both teachers and pupils adhered to.

The empowerment of teachers

One of the strongest impressions I received from my conversations with teachers about the ADS was the increased sense of empowerment they had gained. This emanated from two sources: firstly, through the manner in which the whole school discipline system had been researched, adapted and introduced by the teachers themselves, giving them ownership of it and a vested interest in making it work; and secondly, through the renewed authority the teachers were given through the institutional support of a common discipline framework and through the back up facilities put in place to validate and reinforce their authority. I suspect that this feeling of empowerment may be one of the strongest advantages of an institutional support system: the pervasive ethos of an ethical structure that underpins the teacher's work. As one teacher said: '. . . that is what the pupils expect [back up for the teacher from senior management]. They don't expect you to be on your own any more' (Wilson, 2001).

Drawbacks to the system – from the teachers' point of view

The 'problem' of consistency

I know what to expect, the kids know what to expect. That's very important. Whereas before, you set your own rules, you set your own standards, and in a way you were fighting because you didn't know whether everybody else was setting the same standards, whereas at least now we're working towards the same requirements.

[Q: summing up the previous section of the discussion]: So are you saying then that within the system every teacher must have the freedom to inter- pret that according to their own relationship with the kids . . . and their knowledge . . .?
Teacher: Yes I think so. And with their needs as well. Yes, absolutely, or I think, otherwise don't you run the risk of becoming sort of mechanical, mechanistic in our attempts to cudgel within the human being their behaviour? They're complex things, aren't they? I don't think you can be too mechanistic and remain human, and temper what we do with common sense.

(Teachers, Wilson, 2001)

It is an example of the irony of all complex human affairs that the element in the ADS that had most attracted teachers to it proved to be its Achilles' heel. Teachers had sought the security afforded by a common system of rules and common structures of rewards and sanctions. To remain 'common' the system had to be applied consistently across departments and individual teachers. Consistency proved elusive.

My own feedback to the school, the report submitted by the external moni- tors and the teachers themselves, all confirmed that teachers were not apply- ing the system consistently. They differed in the importance they attached to individual rules, in the frequency of rewards, in the application of the sanctions system, in the interpretation of emergencies for which they would use the back up provisions. The handling of two commonly cited transgressions will serve as examples, one relatively trivial, one more serious. How would you, for instance, deal with pupils who do not come properly equipped for school; and pupils who swear at you or throw things at you? Many teachers spontaneously mentioned to me what I have termed the 'pen syndrome' and how they would deal with pupils who come without pens, pencils or rulers. Coming properly equipped for lessons is one of the school rules, posted up in every classroom. Here are a selection of teachers' responses to transgressions of this rule:

> I mean, if they haven't got a pen, I just say, well, it's your loss of a credit [first level of sanction], and we carry on.

> Pens do run out. When you come to lesson seven, it's quite possible for a kid to have a pen in the morning and it's run out, so I usually allow that one. Okay, maybe with year seven I'm harder with that at first, just to try and establish it, but I feel it's necessary. But when it comes to year ten or eleven, if they haven't got a pen, just lend them a pen. For goodness sake, there's other things you've got to worry about.

> Occasionally, a child will say to me, 'I haven't got a pen.' 'Where is it?' 'I lost it.' 'Fair enough, here's your pen. Borrow mine. Give it to me at the end of the lesson.' Occasionally, I'll even say . . . well, if I know the kid, if it's maybe run out in my lesson, 'Here's a pen. Give it back to me at the end of the day.' Because I know that if that kid goes into other classrooms, although he's had a pen at nine o'clock in the morning, if he goes into other classrooms, they'll say, 'No pen, name' [indicating first level of sanctions] and it's not altogether his fault.
>
> (Teachers, Wilson, 2001)

From this simple example, it becomes clear that teachers' attitudes to rules and how to apply them are fraught with complexities. Another rule states that pupils should treat the teacher and each other, and other people's property with respect. Several teachers mentioned occasions when pupils had either sworn at them or thrown missiles such as coins or sweets. Here is a selection of responses to such incidents:

> Somebody swore at me last week, and I sent him out. [The class had been asked to do a particular task] and he says 'Oh, bloody hell.' So I didn't think that was on.

> I've had, for example . . . a boy who has come back to the school after being suspended for a long time, into the school, sat in the class, and he

said, 'Fuckin' 'ell.' And I said, 'I don't accept that in my classroom', and he looked at me, and I said, 'Where should you be going right now?' And he said, 'Remove.' I said 'Right, you know it's unacceptable, you know I don't like it, well, we'll not say remove this time. I just don't want to hear it again. If it happens again you know what will happen.' 'Sorry, Miss.' And it hasn't happened again . . . Many people would say, 'Right, out!'

If I find him doing that again [throwing sweets at the teacher] because it has happened before, and I know it was him, I will send him out to remove . . . I think he has to learn that you can't go around hurling missiles at the teacher, however small they are.

(Teachers, Wilson, 2001)

So, can it be concluded that some teachers are simply bloody-minded and refuse to follow the common guidelines for the sake of it? Or, is it necessary to ask important questions about why teachers, who support the principle of consistency and common structures, find it so difficult in practice to apply these guidelines?

The need for 'a system with a human face'

I think some people say, well that's the system, use it. If there are problems it's because of the way you're using it. I could go along with that as well. I think you can create problems for yourself if you do start deviating from that, but I still think everybody must make it a human . . . must make it theirs, otherwise you wouldn't be able to stick to something . . . but there again, I do agree there has got to be this consistency, otherwise it wouldn't work.

(Teacher, Wilson, 2001)

Teachers were torn between two apparently antithetical principles: consistency and flexibility. They recognized pupils' need for secure behavioural boundaries; at the same time they recognized that pupils also had individual needs and motivations, which were sometimes expressed in inappropriate behaviour when those needs were not being met. They claimed the professional freedom to deal with those pupils in accordance with their judgement of the context of their behaviour:

[in answer to a question about flexibility] I mean, this is going to sound like a cop out, but you have to, I think, rely on the professional judgement of teachers. I mean, we're the ones in the classroom who have to do the job, and we have to do the best we can using whatever systems we can, and if we have to adapt it a little bit, or use it in a slightly different way to how perhaps we're meant to do it, then that's the way it has to be done.

(Teacher, Wilson, 2001)

One teacher quoted above, for instance, judged that the boy who had already been in remove for swearing was not likely to respond to being sent there again for the same reason. Another teacher withdrew the sanction of remove after the girl in question had apologized voluntarily and they had had the opportunity to discuss the full circumstances of the outburst. These teachers modified the literal application of the system after looking at the situation from the pupils' points of view. Other teachers used the rule of thumb 'Will it work?' when considering particular sanctions for specific individuals. If the answer was no, they found some other way of dealing with the behaviour in question.

These teachers feared that a too narrow interpretation of the ADS would result in many pupils escalating up the sanctions ladder too rapidly and finding themselves in remove for what were in effect a number of trivial offences. They advocated the use of common sense in applying the system, but as can be seen in the examples given of disparate attitudes to pupils who are without pens, common sense is elusive. Teachers handle situations from highly subjective standpoints according to their own perceptions and priorities.

Such flexibility in interpreting the ADS was not, however, approved by all teachers. Some saw the inconsistencies that emerged in the application of the system as undermining it for everyone; and those teachers who did use flexibility did so with a certain amount of guilt. Other teachers apparently had little difficulty in applying the system to the letter, but when further questioned, they also revealed inconsistencies based on their own professional judgement of what was likely to work in specific contexts. There was also a tendency amongst some experienced teachers to regard the ADS as appropriate to those who were too inexperienced or too soft as disciplinarians to create and insist upon their own structures, whilst stronger teachers could continue in their own style.

There was a strong undercurrent of belief that classroom management should be based on creating and preserving good relationships with pupils and on providing for them interesting and relevant learning opportunities. Where the ADS promoted good relationships, it was embraced. Where it was felt to detract from these, it was rejected. The precise circumstances in which the system was experienced as furthering or inhibiting good relationships was likely to differ from teacher to teacher and from class to class.

So where does that leave structured behavioural systems, such as Assertive Discipline, which rely on consistency of application? Later in this book I shall be arguing for an approach to school discipline that is based on consistency of values and standards, articulated through widespread discussion and consultation, guidelines for the implementation of rewards and sanctions that are not too prescriptive and that respect the professional judgement of teachers in their precise application.

The ADS has been described here in the context of support provision for teachers. But in what sense can it be considered as supportive, if so many teachers found it impossible to apply the system consistently? Was it only supportive for those, as some suggested, who were too inexperienced or too weak to manage classes from the strength of their own personalities? My conversations with teachers suggested that the support appeal of the ADS was widespread, but arose less from the precise detail of the system than from the attitudes that underpinned it, namely that classroom management was no longer to be regarded as the sole business of each individual teacher within their own classroom, with failure in this respect marking them out as incompetent teachers. There was a recognition that classroom discipline was a very complex affair, with experienced as well as inexperienced teachers sometimes experiencing problems. It was an attempt to frame a school-wide set of values, which informed the operation of the school and provided an authority that existed beyond the individual personalities of the teachers whilst validating and reinforcing the authority of the teacher when necessary.

It is significant that when the ADS was dismantled after a change in school leadership, the elements that many teachers most regretted losing were the consistency of a common framework and the structures that had been there specifically to support teachers, such as the instant access remove facility, the school-wide detention system and the on-call system. Far from feeling that an institutional authority supported them, the teachers again felt on their own.

The reward system

In common with many whole school behavioural systems based on behaviourist principles, the ADS stressed the rewarding of appropriate behaviour through a rising scale of positive reinforcements, in this case a system of credits leading to certificates of ascending value culminating in the individual's name being entered in a prize draw. At the same time, it was recognized that the issuing of the certificates afforded teachers the opportunity to give the positive recognition, the metaphorical 'pats on the back', which pupils value so much. Teachers widely welcomed the positive aspects of the ADS. It had been recognized that the good behaviour of the majority of pupils went largely unsung, and that teachers' attention was often so exercised by the disruptions to lessons that they often failed to acknowledge the positive efforts of individuals. The structured rewards system reminded them to do so:

> Well I like it [the ADS] . . . I know that pupils want merits; they want a reward; they want to be told, as we all do, that they're doing a good job

... We all respond to being told that we do things well, and I think, to be honest that the rewards are more important than the sanctions. We should be handing out more bits of paper saying: well done.

I love the positive side of it, letters home to parents saying: you know your kid's a nice kid, but here's a letter confirming that we think she's a nice kid, too.

(Teachers, Wilson, 2001)

But there was some disagreement about the nature of the rewards, with some teachers happy with the idea of material rewards and others feeling that it gave out wrong messages:

... but our kids are so materialistic that I wonder whether the sort of prizes our school can financially offer kids are the sort of prizes [they appreciate] ... I do believe that governmentally it's to do with prizes for good work, or money, money rewards for good work, and nothing to do with just doing it, doing it for yourself ... [I use praise] loads of it. Loads of it, and I think praise is often better than prize.

Morally I think it's wrong. I don't like using blackmail with kids. I don't like saying: if you behave then you'll get ... and if you don't behave, this is the consequence. I believe you do that far more subtly with people than just giving material rewards.

(Teachers, Wilson, 2001)

It is ironic, in the face of the evident value that pupils place on the non-materialistic, relationship-based acknowledgement of good or improved behaviour, that the rewards system at Eastbank School was later strengthened to incorporate a token economy of credit cards redeemable at certain outlets in the city.

There were, apparently, deep philosophical divisions in teachers' attitudes towards the ADS. Most teachers were happy to accept the behaviourist basis for the system while wanting it applied in accordance with the more humanistic principles of regard for individual circumstances and motivations; but a few rejected entirely the external manipulation of human behaviour that is implied in behaviourism, in favour of methods of managing pupil behaviour that draw on the power of human relationships and the skills of the teacher in helping pupils to make positive choices. These are not superficial differences. They must be confronted and worked through to enable individual teachers to give wholehearted commitment to a whole school discipline structure.

Pupils' perceptions of the ADS

'Without rules people would just do owt' (pupil, Wilson, 2001). In Part I, I described classroom relationships from the pupils' point of view. In this section I focus more specifically on what pupils said or implied about the Assertive Discipline System.

Most pupils I interviewed agreed that rules were necessary. Some individuals disagreed with specific rules, such as the one forbidding eating and drinking during lessons, but these objections tended to be flippantly expressed and were not upheld by others. Any reservations expressed were less to do with the rules themselves than with the way in which the system was sometimes implemented. Pupils clearly perceived that teachers differed in the importance they attached to particular rules and the action taken when rules are broken. Their attitude did not seem to be one of confusion. They knew and accepted the school rules and the potential consequences of disobeying the rules, but recognized that some teachers enforced the rules more rigorously than others.

On the whole, they thought the consequences laid down by the system were reasonable, but tended to resent having those consequences imposed on them if they sincerely believed that they were undeserved and resulted from the teacher's misreading of a situation. The mere knowledge of the rules and the consequences of flouting them is not enough in itself to prevent some pupils from misbehaving, since so many conflicting emotions, pressures and motivations are at work in determining a pupil's response to the classroom situation. As the pupils themselves said, they would sometimes deliberately misbehave to get themselves put in detention to be with friends, or to look hard. Others said they tried to be sent to remove to get away from the classroom because of particular pupils or particular lessons that they found hard. Some were bored in remove, but others found the calm and orderliness of remove more conducive to work.

In Part I, I commented on pupils' hazy understanding of the reward structure, confusing the credits and certificates given for good behaviour with the merits that rewarded good work. They did not seem able to link the earning of credits with specific evidence of good behaviour in the same way that they could link a particular sanction with an incident of infringement of the rules. It is perhaps because the accruing of rewards results from a negative: absence of bad behaviour is rewarded rather than aspects of good behaviour; whereas single items of bad behaviour are marked by a specific consequence. This interpretation was reinforced when I observed in classrooms. Whereas, for completely understandable reasons, teachers attended to and commented on items of inappropriate or disruptive behaviour, specific instances of good or improved behaviour were much less likely to be commented on during the course of the lesson, because they did not interrupt the flow of the lesson and challenge the teacher's authority.

Pupils respond well to all the positive, interpersonal ways of reinforcing appropriate behaviour: the nods and smiles, the explicit praise, the communication of good or improved behaviour to other, significant, teachers and to parents. And these are the non-concrete, non-material ways of rewarding pupils, which teachers so often lack the time or the emotional space to deliver. Yet even pupils' positive response to these interpersonal marks of approval are not without paradox, because in certain groups, if praise from the teacher is given too openly, the pupil is downgraded in the eyes of peers, and has to misbehave even more decisively to regain street credibility. How sensitive teachers have to be in their handling of all the complexities of the classroom situation!

I am not wishing to denigrate the value of the more concrete rewards for appropriate behaviour: the credits, the certificates and the prize draw. As teachers themselves said, the issuing of these marks of approval gave them the opportunities to acknowledge appropriate behaviour, which were often missing during the course of the lesson. It gave heads of house the opportunity to praise pupils, and it gave parents the opportunity to add their pleasure and approval. But the real influence on pupils' behaviour may well be the positive attention and recognition that accompany the tangible reward, rather than the reward itself. Using one teacher's expression: the praise may be more important than the prize, and perhaps more could be done to maximize the former.

Discussion

I have given some insights into the rationale of whole school behavioural systems in general and described one school's attempts to introduce such a system. The general issues involved are to do with the reasons why many schools have felt the need for a structured approach to matters of school and classroom behaviour, and the tension that is thus revealed between the needs of the collective and the needs of the individual.

The whole school approach represents one response to the great insecurity experienced by many teachers and many pupils to do with what is and what is not acceptable behaviour. In an epoch when the unquestioned moral certainties of a single religious interpretation of life to regulate our dealings with one another have been lost, a whole school system of ethics, based on common values widely discussed and agreed in the school community and the community it serves, offers a strong authoritative moral underpinning to the interactions of all, adults and pupils, in the school.

In place of the multiple individual authorities of each teacher, based on their own personal values, and dependent on the strength of personality of individuals, a whole school system of ethics provides a strong authority to reinforce and validate the work of each teacher. Individual teachers are no longer working in a moral vacuum, but represent the collective ethical authority on which they can draw when necessary. However, if this ethical framework is to have the necessary force, and claim the adherence and commitment of the majority who have to work within it, then it must reflect the will of the majority. A system devised by experts external to the school will not command the same commitment. An internally devised and respected system, reflecting the values of the particular community, must not be allowed to become ossified by custom. It must constantly be renewed and scrutinized, and newcomers to the school community, adults, pupils and parents, need to have the opportunity to discuss it, internalize it and commit themselves to it.

The ways in which the ethical values underpinning relationships within the school are to be interpreted and encouraged in the day to day behaviour of individuals must themselves be consistent with those ethical values they seek to instil. Ways in which teachers seek to ensure compliance in the classroom cannot themselves offend the ethical framework. Teachers may not seek to encourage respect for themselves and others by methods that do not themselves respect pupils. Hence the observations of the pupils quoted in Part I who said they wanted teachers to listen to them, to talk to them in a different way, in short, to respect them and to try to understand the problem from their points of view. However, in practice, situations arise in the classroom in which emotions run high and teachers do not always behave towards pupils in the ways they should. This needs to be recognized within the ethical system and support for the teacher built into the system. This need for recognition that human relationships are often volatile, and that our own personal authority is not always sufficient to influence particular individuals or groups, lies behind teachers' requests for time out facilities for pupils, which are instantly accessible, and for back up facilities for themselves when their own authority needs validation and reinforcement from the collective system.

Celebrating relationships

Good teaching and good classroom control are dependent on the quality of relationships between teacher and pupils.

I think in life we do an awful lot through relationships.

They [teachers] can't possibly build relationships. It's not that they're not. They can't possibly put the effort into building relationships because it [the ADS] takes away the relationship building. It should make it, in some ways, easier, but a lot of discipline in the past has been done through working up to a solution, not just obeying a set of rules . . .

(Teachers, Wilson, 2001)

It can be seen that a system that becomes too inflexible meets the needs of neither pupils nor teachers. Consistency in the values underpinning behaviour for both teachers and pupils lies at the heart of a whole school discipline system. But consistency that does not take account of the particular circumstances in which incidents occur or the judgement of the teacher regarding how best to handle the incident becomes inflexibility, and may alienate pupils who feel that they are being misunderstood or unfairly treated; while too great a leeway for flexibility risks being perceived as licence for a free for all.

Eastbank teachers talked of 'giving the system a human face', of each teacher 'making it their own', of using common sense or professional judgement in applying the system. The fear seems to be that the mechanistic application of rules and sanctions detracts from the art of the teacher in devising creative ways of managing a situation (*cf* A Hargreaves, 1994). Moreover, one teacher's common sense is another teacher's misjudgement. Clearly there is a fundamental tension here between the need for security and consistency on the one hand and the need for a considered and creative response on the other; the demands of the collective, which favours a common structure, and the demands of autonomy, which favours flexibility and individual professional judgement.

Many teachers view good relationships as the key to both good behaviour management and good teaching, and fear that too mechanistic an interpretation of the discipline system could impede the establishment of these relationships. Each school must find its own way to resolve these tensions while incorporating the paradoxical needs. If a highly structured whole school discipline system is seen as a slick, time-saving means of controlling classes, which is automatic and requires little thought and interaction on the teacher's part, it risks becoming the mechanistic, routinized and bureaucratic set of procedures teachers fear.

Clearly, time has to be built into the system as an essential feature: time for the initial negotiations about values and standards and for the regular review of the system; but time also for teachers to resume control of the situation once the tensions that may have resulted in help being summoned or the removal of a pupil have subsided; time for listening and talking, for negotiation.

Crucial to the establishment of a classroom atmosphere in which good relationships can be established is the concept of emotional space. Teachers need to feel relaxed in their classrooms in order to feel in control. They need to be able to take a step back, when confrontation looms, in order to cool the situation and find more constructive solutions. Support is as much about facilitating the establishment of such a classroom ethos as it is about providing big gun back up when relationships break down. The next chapter describes provisions that may help teachers to achieve the time and emotional space to be fully human in their classrooms.

A suggested framework

As a talking point I would like to propose the following as the basis for a possible whole school structure:

- widespread consultation within the school and the surrounding community about the core values that should underpin the work of the school;
- a list of basic rules for the pupils, which operationalize these core values – not too specific, so that they can be adapted to suit different teaching contexts;
- a list of basic principles, which should guide the handling of pupils by teachers and other adults;
- guidelines on reinforcing and rewarding appropriate pupil behaviour, including reminders about all the interactional and relationship-orientated rewards that pupils find valuable; a range of tangible rewards to be awarded;
- a range of sanctions – if possible related to the misdemeanour – to be deployed as considered appropriate by the class teacher;
- support facilities for teachers including instant access time out facilities and access to immediate help when required.

Reviewing discipline procedures

Schools might like to review their discipline procedures by considering the following questions:

- Do you have a whole school discipline policy?
- How did you arrive at this policy? Who was involved in discussing and drawing up the policy?
- Is there room to widen the range of consultation in reviewing the policy?
- What are the values on which the discipline policy is based?
- How do you ensure that pupils are aware of the rules for behaviour and the values they incorporate?
- How do you reinforce appropriate behaviour?
- How do you deal with inappropriate behaviour?
- What provisions are there to support pupils in their behaviour?
- How do you ensure that all teachers are aware of the values underpinning the work of the school?
- How do you support teachers in practising and encouraging these values in their day-to-day interactions with pupils and with each other?
- What facilities are available to teachers in dealing with inappropriate behaviour?
- How does the discipline policy cater for teachers' differences in perception and handling of inappropriate behaviour?

The ADS as a support provision

Eastbank teachers made it clear that the process of consultation and collaboration in constructing their discipline system offered them individually tremendous support. They had the opportunity to discuss openly discipline problems that in the past they had had to suppress, and they began to realize that they were not alone in experiencing these difficulties. As well as receiving support, they were in a position to support others in implementing the system. There were the beginnings of a fundamental change in the way in which teachers perceived discipline and in their attitudes to colleagues who had problems in managing classrooms. There was no longer an automatic equation of bad management equals bad teaching. It was becoming recognized that teaching around 30 individuals at the same time and managing the needs of all of them commands a whole spectrum of skills and predispositions and situational conditions, not all of which can be equally at the disposal of every individual teacher all the time.

In the next chapter I look at other initiatives that draw on teachers' capacities for supporting each other and for collaborating in collective organizational development initiatives. Before I do so, it is appropriate to look briefly at the provision that superseded the instant access remove facility incorporated into the ADS, namely the on-site pupil withdrawal unit.

On-site behavioural units

When Eastbank School dismantled its Assertive Discipline System, the instant access remove facility was replaced with a longer-term behavioural unit, where particularly difficult pupils were placed for several weeks at a time. Pupils went through a standard referral procedure before being placed in the unit, which could take some time. Members of the middle and senior management teams were timetabled to staff the unit. The objectives in referring pupils to the unit were to modify behaviour and to attend to curriculum difficulties that might be contributing to classroom behaviour.

In the limited exploration of the unit which I undertook at the school's request, attitudes of both staff and pupils were largely favourable. Pupils in particular liked the fact that the groups were small and they could get more help with their work; and felt that the teaching and work ethos were better than in mainstream classes. Teachers liked being free from some of the most difficult pupils for a while, but, significantly, did not find that it solved behavioural problems in mainstream classes appreciably: pupils tended to be queuing up for an available place in the unit.

Clearly, there are questions to be asked about the dynamics of mainstream classes that produce a steady stream of potential referrals to the behavioural unit. The unit had not been operating long at the time I was conducting my research. The teachers who staffed it were still exploring different approaches to supporting the pupils while in the unit, and there was concern about the quality of the work they were being given to do. There was also concern about their progress once they were returned to mainstream and about the availability of follow up support.

The implications of on-site units concern:

- whom they are intended to support: teachers or pupils or both;
- the fact that other difficult pupils take the place of those who have been referred to the unit;
- the significance of the fact that pupils in the unit find the atmosphere more conducive to work and to appropriate behaviour, and appreciate the extra help and attention they receive;
- how continuity might be achieved between the unit and mainstream classes;
- whether staffing resources employed in the unit are used more advantageously there than in offering the support in mainstream classes;
- since, to be fair to the pupils concerned, referrals to the unit need to follow a standard procedure, what provision is there for an immediate time out facility.

Although the existence of the on-site behavioural unit was broadly welcomed by staff it was at the expense of other provisions that teachers had found particularly supportive. It took staff out of the general pool of teachers available to support in mainstream classes, and it did not provide the safety net of an instant, short-term remove facility to allow both teachers and pupils emotional space, before conflict became inevitable or damaging.

Clearly, different support provisions meet different needs and a range of support is required to allow both teachers and pupils to interact in mutually fulfilling ways.

4　A second pair of eyes

Adult classroom support

> My initial reaction when somebody says 'support' is having another person in the classroom, sometimes a teacher's aide, sometimes another member of staff, either from this department or elsewhere, who will help those children who need it. If a teacher's aide comes, they usually concentrate on the child or children they are responsible for, but not exclusively. They will always go round and help others as is necessary.
>
> (Teacher, Wilson, 2001)

Amongst the causes of teachers' feelings of stress, inadequacy and failure are the lack of time to attend to all the pupils' classroom needs, and the lack of emotional space to remain relaxed, in control and able to respond appropriately to situations that arise. In the words of pupils: 'there's always too much stuff going on'. In classrooms with a wide range of ability, or where there are significant numbers of pupils with special learning or behavioural needs, teachers become overwhelmed in the attempt to give individual attention to each pupil. Even with graded curriculum materials, there are often substantial numbers of pupils in the class who continue to find the work too difficult for them. They cannot read the instructions properly, or they cannot translate instructions into action, or they cannot retain verbal instructions long enough to put them into operation. Often they just need to be kick-started every so often to keep them engaged. Where the teacher is unable to give the attention quickly enough, pupils become bored and restless and disruption is likely to follow. This may well snowball.

Eastbank teachers welcomed the in-class support they received from a range of adults in a variety of support roles. The school had developed several initiatives for employing extra adults in the classroom:

- teacher's aides and child support assistants;
- a traveller support team;
- a support teacher scheme;
- science and technology technicians.

In their statements to me, teachers drew no particular distinction between qualified teachers working in a support capacity and teacher's aides and child support assistants. The crucial supportive element seems to be the presence of other adults in the classroom. Significantly, pupils also felt that having more adults around would help their behaviour. The role of adult guidance in the lives of children and young people cannot be overestimated, I suspect, and must not be devalued.

To teach or not to teach – the role of classroom assistants

The Eastbank teachers I interviewed were overwhelmingly appreciative of the support they received from classroom assistants, and wanted more of them. Nevertheless, the issues surrounding the employment of classroom assistants are controversial, particularly with regard to their precise duties. Should or should they not be allowed to teach groups of pupils or whole classes? There is clearly a potential danger of role confusion between teachers and classroom assistants. The teaching unions tend to be suspicious about the increasing use of classroom assistants, perceiving it as a way of obtaining teachers on the cheap. Some researchers into mainstream provision for pupils with special educational needs question the effectiveness of employing non-qualified staff with these pupils (British Educational Research Association [BERA] Conference, 2002, anecdotal evidence). Teaching assistants themselves may be ambivalent about taking on increased responsibilities. One classroom assistant whom I interviewed was quite clear that she enjoyed her role as it was: being responsible for helping individuals or very small groups of pupils; she had no desire to train as a teacher or to take on the responsibilities of a teacher: 'It's one of the reasons I didn't go into teaching, because there's too much responsibility, too much paperwork' (Wilson, 2001).

One would have to question a redefinition of a classroom assistant's role that gave him or her more of the teaching and relegated the class teacher to paper shunting and number crunching. But equally, one would have reservations about a redefinition that included more of the clerical and administrative tasks at the expense of close relationships with pupils. My conversations with classroom assistants suggest that, just as in the case of teachers, these relationships provide classroom assistants with their job satisfaction.

Such scenarios may well be extreme interpretations of the revised roles of teacher and classroom assistant. But they do highlight the ambivalences that have developed around the boundaries between them. The case of a school such as Eastbank, which has developed predominantly good relationships between teachers and classroom assistants, suggests that the boundaries should not be too inflexibly demarcated, but it is better left to individuals to decide how best they work together. In the next few sections I describe in more detail how Eastbank teachers relate to the different kinds of classroom support available to them.

Teacher's aides and child support assistants

> She [classroom assistant] comes in specifically for the statemented pupil, but it is very rare for a support teacher or a teacher's aide to restrict themselves to one child. On the whole, I have nothing but praise for that side of support. I have always tried to treat support teachers, teacher's aides, whatever, as complete equals, and I try to make that clear to pupils as well, and we stand back to back as equals, as it were. So I like to feel that I have a good relationship with them, and in that sense, it's always worked within the classroom.
>
> (Teacher, Wilson, 2001)

The distinction between teacher's aides and child support assistants was one of salary level and extent of responsibility. Teacher's aides were paid more and were allowed to take the initiative in preparing programmes of work for children who had a special needs statement, whereas the child support assistants implemented the programmes devised by the teacher. But the teacher's aides were already an endangered species, and future appointments to the school would be for child support assistants only, for reasons of cost. For the purposes of this book, I do not distinguish between teacher's aides and child support assistants, referring to them all as classroom support assistants.

The appointment of classroom support assistants was part of the provision for pupils with statements of special educational needs. Eastbank School operated several systems for supporting pupils. There was a learning support unit, which withdrew pupils for literacy skills once or twice a week. Previously, pupils had also been withdrawn for help in numeracy skills, but staffing levels no longer allowed this to happen. For most of their timetable, pupils with special needs were integrated into mainstream classes. Those who had received a statement of special educational needs had the help of the teacher's aide or child support assistant.

The teachers and the classroom support assistants I spoke to were positive about the mutual relationships that had developed between teachers and classroom assistants. There had been some resistance to begin with before teachers became used to having another adult in the classroom and before they knew precisely what the role of the classroom support assistant was to be. Naturally some teachers were more at ease in the situation than others. But generally speaking, teachers were so stretched that they were just pleased to have the support. There was a widespread feeling amongst both teachers and classroom assistants that much more classroom support was needed:

The only thing I'm not happy with is . . . I think that nowadays the type of learning difficulties that we're getting in, and the lower educational abilities of a lot of the children that we're getting in, there should be more support.

(Classroom assistant, Wilson, 2001)

Well, in this school, I think the thing that's really now standing out is that we have a lot of kids who find it difficult to read, who have problems and, I think, certainly in our department, we need two people in a classroom, especially when you're doing active learning sessions, and I think you'd probably find that colleagues would say that in other areas as well.

(Teacher, Wilson, 2001)

The teachers and the classroom assistants confirmed that although the support assistant was appointed for a specific pupil with special educational needs, a one-to-one mode of working with this child was not always the best for the statemented child or for the class teacher. The statemented child might resent being singled out for individual support. There might be other pupils in the class group who were in the process of being assessed as requiring special help, or there might be individuals who posed particular management difficulties for the teacher who could do with special attention. In practice, therefore, the teacher and the classroom support assistant worked out between them the most effective way of employing the support, with the proviso that the interests of the statemented pupil took priority. Class teachers were very positive in their appreciation of the difference an extra adult made to the ethos of the class and the effectiveness of the lesson:

I know that because we have large groups in the middle years, there are some children who desperately need a lot of help and I just never get to them, or if I do get to them, it's very briefly in the lesson. If I know there's another adult in the room there to help that child or a group of children, I know they're getting more support and motivation . . . They often get to the point where they don't know what to do, and because I haven't got time to get to them, they can sit there for quite long periods of time and get no help at all, and it's just another wasted lesson.

(Teacher, Wilson, 2001)

Ultimate responsibility for classroom management and for disciplining individual pupils within the formal structure of the Assertive Discipline System lay with the class teacher, although the classroom support assistant might intervene with the teacher's consent where pupils directly under her supervision were behaving badly. However, some of the teachers with whom I talked had a broader view of the invaluable role the classroom support assistant played in the informal management of a class simply through being an extra pair of eyes to spot incipient trouble or a pupil who needed help:

You get some kids, who when they've finished a task will start behaving badly because they're bored and have nothing to do; or they just sit there and do nothing; and they need somebody just to kick-start them and say: 'Off you go again, do that.' It might be on the sheet or whatever: now do that; but they don't read it, or they read it and don't see it; and it's not because they're naughty, it's because they somehow can't read it. There's that, but there's also the fact that they can't translate instructions into actions.

[When I'm concentrating on one child] I find it difficult to concentrate on the rest of the group in general, and sometimes just that other pair of eyes helps, if they can just say, stop that, or just a look . . .

(Teachers, Wilson, 2001)

Sometimes the non-teaching person can pick up things that the teacher just can't.

(Classroom assistant, Wilson, 2001)

On the other hand, the classroom support assistant has a prior responsibility to the statemented pupil, and at times the atmosphere of the classroom is not helpful to his or her relationship with that pupil. In these circumstances the support assistant will perhaps opt to withdraw the child, and one or two others who need help, from the whole class situation.

Clearly there is a whole area of formal and informal discipline that needs to be discussed and agreed upon between the support assistant and the class teacher. The potential for role conflict is there and becomes even more evident when a support teacher is working with a class teacher. I shall discuss this issue further.

Good communication between support assistant and class teacher becomes crucial for the smooth running of the partnership. The teachers and support assistants spoke of the necessity for time to pre-plan lessons and activities so that the support assistant could contribute expertise in the design of materials for pupils with special needs and plan how she could best organize her work for a specific lesson. They all regretted that they made too little time to do this:

I do feel there could be some improvements made, mainly the communication between the support assistant and the staff as to what work is going to be done in a particular lesson. And also, it's much better if the support assistant has pre-knowledge of the particular worksheets that they're going to be working from, or which particular subjects they're going to cover, and any differentiated material that's going to be used.

(Classroom assistant, Wilson, 2001)

Where it falls down, perhaps [the support system] is – this is a personal confession – we ought to make more time to get to the teacher's aides before they come into the classroom, and say: you're going to do this, that and the other. We always say we will, and we very rarely do.

(Teacher, Wilson, 2001)

Class teachers expressed frustration that the support assistant sometimes could not attend the lesson when expected, upsetting the teacher's plans and organization for that lesson. It sometimes happened when the specific child the support assistant was allocated was absent, and the assistant was directed elsewhere in the school. If the support was focused solely on the child with special needs, this would not pose a problem for the class teacher, but where, as often happened, the support assistant was relied upon to give attention to other pupils in the class, class teachers could find themselves suddenly without an expected source of support.

Already, when I conducted the fieldwork between 1995 and 1998, classroom assistants were becoming overstretched and demoralized in the same way as the teachers: 'We're all stretched, all the support staff. We could do with more support . . . If every class could have some sort of aide or child support assistant it would be a wonderful idea . . . and I think it would take some of the stress off the class teacher, and also probably improve standards to some extent' (classroom support assistant, Wilson, 2001).

The situation is unlikely to have greatly improved since then.

Like teachers, classroom assistants need cherishing. They need the conditions in which they can work most effectively. They need appreciation and encouragement. They need a support system of their own and they need status and recognition. Although not all support assistants want to train as fully qualified teachers, they do want some form of training and staff development that acknowledges and extends their particular expertise:

I find the whole area of special needs and learning difficulties fascinating. I do wish in some ways that the staff, the support staff – I'm talking about the teacher's aides and the child support assistants – could maybe go on more INSETS, for dealing with children that have got specific difficulties, how to get across to them, to start them off . . . the trouble here is, that because most of the teachers were secondary trained, they are not particularly equipped to teach the child literacy skills or numeracy skills from the beginning, because a lot of them come here with a reading age of about 8.5 and their numeracy is round about the same, and it's difficult for us to know what techniques to employ to bring the children up . . . I feel that if we had more expertise . . . we've got lots of programmes, but there's a technique to teaching, and I wish sometimes that we had more time to be able to go on a course to explore these techniques . . .

(Classroom assistant, Wilson, 2001)

My informant said that in her local authority there was a course available leading to a qualification, but it was at an unsuitable time of the day when support assistants had home responsibilities.

Classroom assistants often derive their job satisfaction from the close relationships they develop with individual pupils. Although the assistants I spoke with helped class teachers with practical jobs such as mounting work and photocopying, they are likely to resent being formally cast in the role of class dog's body. As I shall discuss later, a range of adult support is required for different kinds of task.

The need for flexibility

My own experience of working with a particular classroom support assistant was entirely positive. Usually we found the time to discuss new topics in time for the classroom assistant to modify worksheets appropriate for the pupil she was mainly concerned with. When the lesson was such that the pupil did not require individual help, the classroom assistant would make herself available to work with groups of pupils, or simply keep an eye on potential disrupters. Occasionally she discreetly made me aware of trouble brewing or pupils in difficulties before I had had a chance to notice and in time for pre-emptive action to be taken. On occasions when I attempted something particularly innovative, which required careful planning and organization, it was invaluable to have another adult in the classroom to work with groups or generally help the pupils orientate themselves in the activities. She always tried to forewarn me when she was not going to attend a particular lesson, but I always missed her when she was not there.

In spite of the dangers of role conflict and misunderstandings between teacher and support assistants, my own experience and my conversations with teachers and with classroom assistants suggest that it might be counter-productive to impose tight boundaries between the roles of teacher and assistant or to ascribe too definitively the specific responsibilities of the support assistant. Certainly there should be guidelines to help frame the relationship between the two, particularly in areas of responsibility where legal accountability is involved, but the details of the interaction should be worked out in practice between the individuals concerned and depend on the particular skills, training and personality of the classroom assistant and where these complement those of the class teacher.

Time, trust, consultation and flexibility seem to be the keywords, here. In a profession traditionally so insular as teaching, the introduction of other adults into what used to be the class teacher's own little empire might seem like introducing a mole into the secret society of the classroom. In the current ethos of accountability, assessment and appraisal, it is important to the teacher that classroom assistants are not there to pass judgement, to gossip about the teacher or to report back to the school management:

They weren't sure what I was going to be doing. They weren't sure whether I was going to be criticizing. But I made it perfectly clear from the start that my role was to support the child that I was with and nothing more. What they were doing was nothing to do with me. They were teaching their subject, and in whatever way they taught it, didn't matter to me. I was there for the child. And gradually they've come to appreciate that with more and more children coming in with more and more problems, they do need the support.

(Classroom support assistant, Wilson, 2001)

However, where the assistant does witness the handling of a pupil in ways that she feels to be profoundly unprofessional or unethical, her own professionalism is put to the test. In such cases, and indeed in any case where a member of staff witnesses serious abusive behaviour against pupils, guidelines for the professional handling of such incidents are essential.

Similarly, classroom assistants should not feel exposed to the criticism of professionals with higher levels of training, skills and salary. Teaching, managing and supporting young people is challenging work for which there are few blueprints. Openly acknowledging the difficulties presented and taking the time to discuss and plan together is likely to create the trust required for collaborative working. One of my themes throughout this book is that the particular conditions of traditional classrooms can create frustrations and tensions, which lead to distorted behaviour in both pupils and teachers. The more adults there are around to share the task of supporting and guiding young people, the greater the likelihood of a benign and wholesome classroom ethos and the less likelihood of overstretched and demoralized teachers or classroom assistants losing control of themselves and acting against individual pupils in ways that are against their professional values and intentions.

Support teachers

... where a member of staff might not necessarily resent a teacher's aide in the room, sometimes they're a bit wary of another member of the [teaching] staff being in the room. But then again, if you've got a good relationship with that person, it works very well because [they] just let me get on with it . . . but I do know people who feel uncomfortable with another person in the room. It never worries me. I do the dog and pony act whoever's there.

(Support teacher, Wilson, 2001)

The use of an additional teacher to work alongside the class teacher differs from the use of classroom assistants in that another qualified teacher can undertake the same level of responsibilities as the class teacher. However, there is also more potential for role conflict and misunderstanding; and more possibility of professional criticism, defensiveness and rivalry.

Eastbank School operated three schemes involving support teachers working alongside class teachers in mainstream classes, all of which elicited a generally favourable response from teachers. These schemes concerned:

- Teachers with qualifications or experience in teaching pupils with special educational needs working to support these pupils in mainstream classes.
- Teachers with specific responsibility for traveller children.
- Teachers on a lighter than normal timetable, who were allocated to support the class teacher in class groups that were known to present difficulties. Faculties could choose to organize this support scheme internally, which ensured that classes were supported by a teacher with the relevant subject knowledge and teaching skills. Otherwise, teachers joined a centrally organized panel and might be allocated to support in any faculty.

Although each of these schemes had a different focus, they were greeted with similar enthusiasm and reservations, presented similar ambivalences and were subject to similar constraints. They can therefore be discussed together.

Teachers generally welcomed the presence of the support teacher, particularly in groups where there were a number of pupils with learning or behavioural difficulties, for all the same reasons that they welcomed the classroom support assistants as an extra pair of hands and eyes to help ensure that all pupils received the attention they needed. The learning support teachers and the traveller support teacher were only expected to be present where there were pupils with specific needs in the group. The teacher support system, which used teachers who had a lighter than average timetable, could be more flexibly deployed, subject to their availability. This scheme was, however, particularly vulnerable to fluctuations in staffing levels. During the period of my main fieldwork, Eastbank teachers regretted that the numbers of teachers who were available for support duties was much diminished in that current year. When I returned to the school two years later to do some follow up work, teachers reported that the amount of support they had received through this scheme had increased for a year and then decreased as teachers were needed for other priorities.

Although classroom support assistants and support teachers felt that class teachers were sometimes wary of their presence in the classroom, the class teachers themselves, almost without exception, expressed no such reservations. The very few hesitations in wholeheartedly endorsing the presence of other adults were to do with teachers' ultimate responsibility for the needs of all pupils as part of their role, and the difficulties possibly presented through teachers supporting in classes where the subject being taught was alien to them. Such reservations highlight the need once again for trust, consultation, negotiation and flexibility in working out the best ways of collaborating for the two teachers concerned. Here is the partnership from the point of view of the support teacher:

> If you're going to ask for more support in the classroom, you've got to be prepared to team-teach . . . it depends how much of an individualist you are. If you find it difficult to have somebody else making the decisions . . . or do you, before you come into the room, have an arrangement like: you are responsible for the discipline, and I'm responsible for seeing that this particular child gets his work done? It's got to be done on an individual basis, and it's got to be done before we start going into the classroom.

> It depends on the confidence of the teacher. I think with any sort of support, the first thing you've got to do is make the teacher feel comfortable and confident when you're in the room. So . . . if I have to act as a teacher's aide for a while, I'm happy to do that to begin with. I think you can usually identify which children are giving concern, and maybe somebody's behaviour might make teaching the class difficult, and that's where you want to target your support really.

> In one instance, I actually teach the class for one of the periods that I support a week, and the class teacher does the support work [by agreement with the teacher].
>
> (Support teachers, Wilson, 2001)

And from the point of view of the class teacher:

> If you definitely know that somebody's going to be with you on a Wednesday morning, then you could perhaps organize your material so that you began a new topic at that particular time, so that when you're introducing something that's quite difficult, it could be introduced to a small group by the [support person] at the same time.

> [Q. How do you use the support?] It depends on the situation, actually, and on the child. In years past there have been children who didn't need that adult with them all the time, so in that case, the adult will go round other members of the class, when the particular child they were with didn't need the help. There's a situation I've had this year where I have quite a difficult group, so we've arranged that when the support teacher comes once a week, she actually takes that child, the one she's supporting, out of the room to a quieter place so they can get on, and she might take another child as well, so there'd be a couple of them. This also may help because the child whom we're talking about can't really cope with the work that the rest of the group are doing, so by

being withdrawn, he can do different work, but he doesn't have the stigma of being given different work.

(Teachers, Wilson, 2001)

As with the classroom support assistants, teachers regret that they don't have enough time to liaise with the support teachers before the lesson:

> It's more off the cuff. When they come in, I tell them what I am doing. If, as happened last week, I was doing a test, so there wasn't really any need to have this person in the lesson, I simply said to the support teacher: I don't really need you this time . . . It's sort of working off the top of your head: what can you do now? How can we cope with this situation? There isn't really time to sit down and discuss or plan what we're going to do over a long time.

(Wilson, 2001)

Support teachers talked of having a wider remit than just working in the classroom alongside the teacher. According to their own particular expertise, they were involved in differentiating worksheets, preparing curriculum materials for general use in the classroom, record-keeping and home–school liaison.

It is significant that Eastbank teachers rarely differentiated between the support teachers and the classroom support assistants when talking about the value to themselves of the support offered. It seems to be the presence of another adult, whatever the precise nature of the role, that class teachers find supportive. Pupils, too, welcome extra adults around, and value the attention they get in smaller groups. All this suggests that the day-to-day interaction with lots of adults in different roles is of great importance, both for the development of young people and for the effective management of class groups. The relationship between one teacher and a class of children can become too intense, stressfully so when the relationship is strained for any reason. The presence of other adults in the classroom may have a generally relaxing effect on relationships, acting as a safety valve for both teacher and pupils.

Personal experience of support teaching and support teachers

I have both worked as a support teacher and experienced working with support teachers in my classroom. My experience of the latter has been mainly positive. I cannot pretend that I ever viewed the prospect of another teacher working in the same classroom as myself with equanimity. Educated and entering the profession in the tradition of one classroom one teacher, the idea of another teacher observing and possibly judging me was daunting. In theory, however, I have always supported the concept of team teaching and believed that the feelings of self-consciousness and possibly competitiveness had to be overcome.

In the most positive of these partnerships, these reservations were quite easily dispelled. The support teacher was there specifically for certain children and focused mainly on them, leaving me the decision-making about the content and conduct of the lesson. But, as in the case of flexible working relationships with classroom assistants, the support teacher would also help with other pupils after consultation with me. I came to regard the support teacher as welcome support for myself as well as for the pupils concerned. She appreciated the difficulties presented by that particular class. Undoubtedly, the success of the relationship between class teacher and support teacher depends on the sensitivity and tact of the supporting teacher.

The reverse role, that of support teacher, was one that I enjoyed. I have worked as a teacher with small groups in the special needs class and in one school, as faculty coordinator of a scheme for helping pupils with special educational needs, I used several free periods a week acting as support teacher where invited to do so by the class teacher. I would leave the decision as to how I might help entirely to the class teacher. Sometimes they wanted me to work with individuals or small groups in the class; sometimes they preferred me to take the pupils out of the class to work with them on the same activities the rest of the class were engaged in. In one year eleven French group, a few pupils were so disrupting the examination class that the teacher wanted them out of the class altogether. I supervised them in my own classroom, trying to overcome their demotivation and resistance by getting them to act out scenes in French and taping them. One of the group became so anxious to continue with the examination course that she was able to negotiate a re-entry to the mainstream class.

In another school, I tried to introduce a similar scheme, involving a rota of staff in the modern languages faculty to be available to receive pupils who were disrupting another lesson and supervising them until the class teacher was free to deal with the pupil. I devised a questionnaire for these pupils, which encouraged them to think about the reasons for exclusion from the class and about how they might make amends, and which they could usefully complete whilst they were out of the class. This had the double advantage of freeing the supervising member of staff from active involvement in the incident and giving the class teacher and the pupil a basis for discussion once the class teacher was available to deal with it. The scheme suffered from a lack of support from some colleagues who felt that discipline was a school matter rather than a faculty matter, and did not wish to volunteer precious free periods. Clearly, much discussion is needed amongst staff about ways of tackling classroom disruption if a consensus is to be reached regarding collaborative ways of supporting colleagues.

During my fieldwork for the research, I tried to repay the time and co-operation that teachers had given me by offering myself as support teacher where this help might be useful. This was accepted in three ways: I spent one afternoon a week as a support teacher in the learning support department alongside other staff supporting pupils who had been withdrawn for a lesson from mainstream classes for extra help in basic literacy skills; I supported for one lesson a week in a year nine class, working with a small group of pupils who normally became disruptive if they were not receiving constant attention; I was used by one teacher to observe specific groups of pupils so that she could obtain a better overall picture of the group dynamics and the relationship of that group to the rest of the class.

These experiences gave me first-hand insights into some of the tensions and ambiguities involved in being a support teacher. I was subjected to some of the same kinds of treatment that class teachers were exposed to. I was sworn at, told to shut up sotto voce, had personally insulting remarks directed at me, had my instructions ignored or flagrantly rejected. I had decisions to make about an appropriate response that did not interrupt the class lesson or circumvent the authority of the teacher. I had to decide what to do about instances of inappropriate behaviour I had witnessed but that had escaped the attention of the class teacher. I had to keep reminding myself that I was there to support the teacher as well as individual or groups of pupils. I must do nothing that would interfere with the teacher's plans for the class, undermine the teacher's authority or add to the pressures of the situation. This was not always an easy role to play, and I did not always feel I was getting it right. Clearly, there must be absolute trust and coincidence of intentions between the class teacher and the support teacher for such a close collaborative situation to be supportive and effective.

Technical and administrative support

It's a practical subject. You need people . . . it's just managing the resources, and more and more subjects are like that. You need a technician for each faculty, or a support person for each faculty, however you want to use that person.

The other way of looking at support . . . is something along the lines of the science department and CDT, where you have got a technician type of person, or an admin assistant, somebody who would give some help with photocopying of worksheets, maybe the preparation of worksheets . . . if there's something that's handwritten to put it on the computer; somebody you could say to: I need a class set of something for tomorrow, and they would be able to make sure that the class set that should be available around the department was available for you, like book it out. There are numerous occasions when you just know you have got to spend next lunch time looking, finding, seeking, counting whatever piece of equipment it is . . .

(Teachers, Wilson, 2001)

Several of the fieldwork participants expressed appreciation of the role of the laboratory and workshop technicians, and mentioned the need for a technician or administrative assistant to work with every faculty, releasing teachers' time from practical chores for more specialist preparation, marking and record-keeping. Eastbank School employed four technicians who were based in the science and technology departments. Theoretically they were available for help with technical equipment in other faculties. In practice, their time was more than exhausted catering for the needs of the new science and technology syllabuses. One technician describes examples of ways of helping across the school if there was more time:

> I was talking to the history teacher the other day, who said: 'It would be good if we had technicians in history.' Why? 'Well we might need videos setting up, and we might need overhead projectors repairing.' He said, 'There's a case in point, the programme, *The People's Century*.' He said he's recorded all of them, and it would be good if someone could sit down and edit the whole series together, taking out the salient points which would back up his work in Twentieth Century History. It would be marvellous to do, theoretically. I've trained as an AV [audio-visual] technician, I could do that, but the demand on my time in science is so great that any free time I have other things to do.
>
> (Technical support staff member, Wilson, 2001)

This technician defined the role as helping teachers to make a difference. Ideally, by being able to take care of equipment and make sure it is in working order when it is needed, the technician removes some of the petty niggles and stresses that build up and 'chip away at your self-confidence'. In reality:

> It is at best haphazard . . . I know that the Modern Languages Department, for instance, have . . . the fact that three or four of their tape recorders are down means that half their equipment is missing, and, ideally, it would be good to say alright, if you bring it over I'll do it now . . . because tape recorders are a major way that languages are taught. And I feel bad about having to put colleagues off . . . so, three or four more technicians in the school would smooth things over.
>
> (Technical support staff member, Wilson, 2001)

The role boundaries of the technician can be very fluid, depending on the particular personality and skills of the individual. One technician was occasionally used in a support capacity with pupils, helping those with learning difficulties to read a test paper, for example. This same person sometimes gave up free time to talk to interested pupils about topic areas in science in which he had particular expertise.

Pupils do not necessarily perceive the same role status differentials and definitions as do the adults. They will relate to whomever they feel will give them the attention and support they need. One technician described incidents where he won the confidence of particularly troubled pupils and was able to counsel and advise. He felt that the fact that he was not a teacher contributed to these young people's trust in him. It can only be beneficial for young people to have a range of adults to turn to for guidance but there are obviously pitfalls here for unwary adults who find themselves caught between the need to respect a young person's confidences and the need to seek professional help for the pupil where necessary. It raises issues about professional development opportunities for all the adults who come into close contact with the pupils.

Summary

The teachers in Eastbank School generally welcomed and appreciated the help offered by the extra adults in a variety of roles who supported their work in the classroom. These adults allowed the teacher to operate more closely to their ideal of being able to give individual attention to more pupils and to respond more appropriately to pupils' social and emotional needs. They were able to relax more in their relationships with pupils and so to be and give out more of themselves. Given that pupils also expressed a need for more adults around the school, the roles and significance of adults in the lives of young people need greater research and consideration.

Amongst the teaching profession as a whole, there have been reservations expressed about the employment of unqualified adults in the classroom. Even the idea of classroom support assistants is not welcomed by everybody. Researchers working with teachers of children with special educational needs tell of unfortunate experiences with untrained support assistants (BERA, 2002, anecdotal evidence), and there is some suspicion in the teaching unions that classroom assistants are a cheap option to employing qualified teachers. These reservations do not invalidate the positive experiences that many teachers have of their classroom support assistants, nor must they detract from the benefit to children and young people of a range of adult role models, and available guidance.

Teachers' traditional attitudes

A more serious barrier to the acceptance by teachers of other adults in the classroom is the one teacher one class tradition. In Part I, I showed how teachers had an ambivalent attitude to their role as sole leader and manager in the classroom, sometimes experiencing this as threatening isolation, sometimes as exhilarating and inspirational performance. Other adults in the classroom inevitably alter the ways in which we can relate to the class as a whole. This may be perceived as liberating, inhibiting, even shaming. What is required, I suggest, is a new way of looking at classroom management difficulties, and a tolerance and flexibility towards colleagues and their preferred ways of working. Just as pupils' sensitivities are respected in determining the ways in which learning support is offered to them, whether in class or through withdrawal, for example, similarly the particular sensitivities of teachers and support individuals should be considered in deciding how best to actualize the support relationship.

Other adults in the classroom

It is significant that it is not just extra teachers that Eastbank teachers found valuable, it was extra adults in a variety of roles. One teacher mentioned the help she had received in another school from a sixth former specializing in her subject who could give attention to individual pupils in her classes. This raises the whole question of how a range of adults including parents and members of the community might be used in the school to work alongside teachers. It also, of course, raises important issues to do with how these extra adults may be inducted into the values and ethos of the school so that everybody feels they are working to the same ends; and it suggests the need for different training and staff development opportunities to equip ancillary staff, including, of course, lunch time and playground supervisors, and volunteer assistants with appropriate skills and information. Above all, it highlights the need to build into the working day of the different adults in the school the time to share information, negotiate roles, discuss programmes of work, share out tasks and in doing all these, to develop the trust that is essential to successful collaboration.

Key ingredients of a successful classroom collaboration

From what class teachers, support teachers, classroom assistants and technicians have said, the key ingredients to a successful collaboration are:

- flexibility – so that teacher and support person can work out the details of the partnership to suit their own specific strengths, the needs of individual pupils and the needs of the class group;
- time – for joint pre-planning, review and for discussion of difficulties or misunderstandings;
- communication – so that each knows what the other is doing;
- trust – in the goodwill of the other and in the willingness of each to work together to solve the problems that arise.

Discussion points

- What kinds of support personnel are available in your school and to you personally?

- What are the criteria for their deployment?
- Are there timetabled opportunities for pre-planning and review meetings?
- Are there differences in the way you work with support teachers and with classroom support assistants?
- Are there training opportunities for classroom assistants 1) out of school 2) in school? What do classroom assistants in your school feel about their training opportunities? What do they feel about their status and their relationships with teachers?
- How do *you* feel about the presence of other adults in the classroom? Analyse the reasons for your feelings.
- Think about your best and worst experiences of working with a support teacher or a classroom support assistant. What were the ingredients that made for the success of one experience, and the factors that impaired the working relationship of the worst experience?
- Have you had experience of supporting in a colleague's classroom? What are the factors that, for you, contribute to a positive experience as a support teacher?
- What opportunities are there in your school for other adults to help in the classroom? Would you welcome it? How might you make use of the extra help? What kinds of training or developmental opportunities do you need to help you accept and utilize other help?
- What kinds of structures are needed in the school to support a range of adult help and allow them to become part of the ethos of the school?

It is clear then, that the provision of adults with qualified teacher status or otherwise to work alongside the class teacher is one important source of support, not only for pupils but also for the teacher. The support offered the teacher resides in the creation of more time to attend to tasks and responsibilities requiring the teacher's specific skills; the reduction in pressure and guilt in knowing that more pupils are being helped in the lesson; the provision of the emotional space to respond more appropriately to the management problems that arise; and the temporary relief from the feelings of isolation that so many of the participants admitted to.

However, the importation of other adults into a situation where traditionally one adult was in sole charge of a classroom of pupils brings with it new ways of working, different kinds of tensions and emotional needs, and these need to be recognized and catered for. This will be discussed in more depth in Part III. The fact that the teachers and support staff in Eastbank School appeared from their statements to work well together in most cases indicates a capacity for collaboration within the school ethos, which is worth exploiting and developing.

Support staff need cherishing. During the period of the fieldwork, covering two OFSTED inspections, support staff showed signs of overwork, stress and decreasing job satisfaction, similar to that expressed by class teachers.

Working with children and young people in whatever capacity often gives great satisfaction, but it is also a source of seemingly insuperable challenge, personal doubt, loss of confidence and self-esteem. The adults in a school are there to support the young. In order to be able to do this effectively, they must also support each other; and support must be part of the very fabric of the institutional structure.

5   Together we stand

Collaboration as support

I miss the self-help group . . . I liked being able to talk things over with others and to listen to problems others were having, and to know others were experiencing similar problems. I liked the mutual support. I think there's a need for that.

(Teacher, Wilson, 2001)

I have already noted the importance that Eastbank teachers attached to the opportunity for collaboration and teamwork which the Assertive Discipline System afforded them. The school developed another important initiative, which involved teachers working together and supporting each other. Whilst broadly welcomed by the staff who participated in it, it also threw up ambivalences, which it is important to explore. In addition, I entered into a collaborative arrangement with a senior member of staff in connection with my research, which involved this peer support initiative. The eventual collapse of this collaboration highlighted many of the issues that can make or mar a successful partnership. The collaboration foundered on a series of misunderstandings. Without in any way attributing blame for its collapse, I use the case as an object lesson for the factors that have to be taken into consideration in setting up a collaborative venture. In this chapter, therefore, I look at two aspects of collective support: peer support and collaborative initiatives.

Peer support

Peer support in the literature

A sense of isolation is a common experience amongst teachers. The literature on teacher support increasingly advocates forms of peer support (Chisholm, 1994; Hanko, 1995; Creese, Norwich and Daniels, 1997a and b). This usually refers to formal groups of teachers specifically set up to offer advice or problem-solving opportunities, rather than to the informal friendship and collegiate networks that arise in staffrooms. This is not to downgrade the importance of the informal collegiate support which a benign school ethos will encourage, or which may even arise despite, or to spite, a conflictual and negative school ethos. One teacher in my research felt that these informal support networks, which arose naturally in the staffrooms, were more effective than formal groups.

Whether formal or informal, it seems that teachers are increasingly needing the shared experience, collective insights and collegiate authority of groups of colleagues to counteract their feelings of isolation, uncertainty and powerlessness in the classroom. It is significant that my research has confirmed the findings of others (for example, Gewirz, 1996) that opportunities for informal peer support are diminishing as teachers spend less time relaxing in staffrooms:

> Comparing it to my first year here [five years previously], there's just no comparison at all, really. Then, there actually seemed to be time to go and sit in the staffroom, and things like that, but it doesn't happen nowadays. You are constantly needing to do something.

> Time spent chatting might seem like wasted time, but in fact is very valuable . . . Peer self-help groups give the opportunity to exchange ideas. The 20 minutes spent chatting in the house block staffrooms used to be invaluable, but this tends not to happen.
>
> (Teachers, Wilson, 2001)

My research also suggests that formal peer support groups are vulnerable to other priorities such as preparation for OFSTED inspections, assessment meetings and the like.

'*Supportive interdependence*' – *a selective review of the literature on peer support*

As indicated above, relationships between teachers may be a crucial factor in determining whether teachers feel supported in managing pupils' behaviour. Endorsed by the Elton Report (1989), peer support, particularly in relation to teachers' responses to challenging or disruptive behaviour in the classroom, has become a potentially fruitful approach to classroom management issues during the past 15 years. As Chisholm (1996) points out, several exponents of peer support (for example, Hanko, 1995) demonstrate its value in reducing teachers' sense of isolation and raising morale through the creation of a climate in which teachers can share their difficulties and make use of the experience of colleagues in a secure, blame-free environment. Since I believe peer support to be an essential ingredient in creating a school ethos in which teachers can function with sanity and humanity, I am devoting some space to describing three different approaches to structuring organized peer support. I shall be referring to the work specifically of Chisholm (1994), Hanko (1995) and Creese, Norwich and Daniels (1997a).

Chisholm – promoting peer support among teachers

Chisholm's paper identifies different approaches to peer support as expounded in the literature, characterized by the use or not of an external facilitator, and whether the focus is on the development of general classroom management skills or on problem-solving related to specific cases. He then describes a two-year project carried out in one authority to promote peer support in the authority's schools. The approach is eclectic, making use of strategies found to be helpful in other projects.

Facilitators, nominated by each participating school, are first trained in the concepts and group management skills associated with peer support. Each is then responsible for promoting peer support projects within their own schools. Importantly, these projects do not follow an externally imposed format, but arise out of the perceived needs of the school and the participating teachers, thus encouraging participant ownership of the projects. As a result, many variants of peer support arise. Chisholm categorizes these as projects that produce policy, projects that enact policy, projects with a classroom research focus and projects that use co-teaching. An exciting spin-off from the projects is the extent to which the initial core project often spawns other developments within the school. One of the most productive outcomes is the formation in several schools of peer support groups, specifically aimed at giving informal support to individual teachers requesting help with behaviour management problems.

Issues that Chisholm identifies as needing to be addressed by the participating schools include:

- differing priorities between head teachers and teachers concerning relative benefits of the project to the school as a whole and to individual teachers;
- differing perceptions between head teachers and teachers about control of professional development initiatives;
- provision of time to facilitate the development of projects;
- promotion of the appropriate ethos to facilitate trust amongst project participants;
- issues of confidentiality and ownership of sensitive information that emerges within the project.

A further issue that he identifies concerns the evaluation of changes in teachers' and pupils' behaviour that actually result from the projects. Teachers' own perceptions testify to the degree of support and increased confidence they receive from the projects, but, like Nias (1989), Chisholm acknowledges that collegial supportiveness can become emotional reinforcement of teachers' current practices:

. . . it would be informative to have received data from schools about the precise nature of the support the teachers gave each other. At a conceptual level it had been clear that skill development would best be promoted through the use of a 'critical friend'. This implies a degree of constructive challenge in the support process – the notion that peers would be able to 'stretch' their colleague's reflection and classroom activity. While it is evident that all teachers enjoyed the security and personal affirmation from time spent working together, we cannot be sure of the degree to which these relationships tested them in a constructive sense.

(p 173)

From the point of view of this book, the following issues are significant:

- the emphasis on school-based, teacher-led projects;
- the developmental nature of the process, through which initial projects spawned others;
- the development of a secure, blame-free ethos in which teachers felt able to admit to difficulties and ask for help;
- the reduction in teachers' feelings of impotence and isolation.

However, the paper also hints at potential obstacles to the success of the projects, arising from lack of priority given to peer support in terms of time, and management attitudes to grassroots initiatives.

Two particular projects are significant for this book in view of the prominence I have given to a whole school behavioural policy. Both combine peer support with the implementation and operation of Assertive Discipline within the respective schools. In the first, the emphasis was on helping teachers to introduce and maintain the system, and in the second school:

where Assertive Discipline was already established, the school tried 'to create a climate in which people feel comfortable in asking for support'. Here the support group meet regularly to help individual teachers with their own concerns, and provide an organised structure for discussions. Simultaneously, the facilitator encouraged the development of an informal peer support network to meet the day-to-day needs of teachers. The project report . . . identifies the development of positive staff relationships, which make it easier for staff to discuss practical issues and arrive with some confidence at personal strategies and solutions.

(p 169)

In these projects there is a recognition that formal structures are not sufficient in themselves to give teachers the support they need. Classroom management difficulties create deep emotional responses in teachers, which, linked with the traditional equation of teacher competence with 'keeping order', form barriers to open admission and discussion of problems. A different perspective on classroom management issues, which acknowledges the ubiquitousness of these and the emotions aroused, is needed as a prerequisite to any support structure.

Hanko – special needs in ordinary classrooms

Hanko has become the doyenne of consultative peer support groups. In a project undertaken in the early 1980s, covering a number of schools in one local authority (Baker and Sikora, 1982, quoted in Hanko, 1995), she explored a specific approach to teacher support. This involved an external consultant in the first place, working with groups of teachers to harness their existing skills more effectively in dealing with pupils with emotional and behavioural needs. The ultimate aim was that the groups should become self-supporting, offering a collective problem-solving approach towards individual cases presented by a member of the group. The objectives of the groups included:

- training, in working through real, individual cases, in the use of problem-solving skills;
- the acknowledgement of the presenting teacher's own experience, skills and previous efforts;
- the space and support, through which teachers may recognize the dysfunctional patterns of attitudes, behaviours and responses that may have arisen in the course of previous efforts to meet the child's needs;
- the maintenance of the presenting teacher's autonomy in making appropriate use of the outcomes of the case discussion;
- the opportunity to follow up individual cases through future discussion;
- the articulation, with the help of the consultant's expertise, of the theoretical underpinnings to individual case discussions, which may have more general application.

The composition of the groups involved in the project ranged from whole school staffs (primary), through interschool groups comprising representatives from several primary schools in an area and year seven teachers from the secondary comprehensive school they fed, to intraschool groups in secondary comprehensives. Although the project was set up to support teachers in dealing with pupils who were presenting considerable emotional or behavioural difficulties, it was also recognized as a support facility for teachers who wished to discuss any difficulties or incidents with specific pupils that arose in the course of their day-to-day classroom interactions. It was acknowledged that interaction with pupils who are difficult to manage causes teachers great emotional distress, which may distort their responses. It was also acknowledged that teachers may have personal difficulties which contribute to their inappropriate responses. It was stressed, however, that the groups are essentially consultative, not counselling groups, with the emphasis on focused professional problem-solving for the benefit of the pupils under discussion, and not therapy groups for the teachers. Nevertheless it was recognized that there were therapeutic benefits to the teachers concerned through enhancement of professional skills and self-confidence.

The following quotation from the project evaluator's report is of particular relevance to this book in indicating what the teachers themselves felt were the benefits of a peer support group:

Comments on questionnaires and informal remarks addressed to the evaluator, together with the latter's own participant observation of some of these meetings, all pointed very strongly to the benefit for teachers of having their cases looked at dispassionately from the 'outside' with the consultant and other staff in the group. The following examples illustrate the gains that teachers felt they had achieved:

'. . . confidence from knowing other teachers have as many doubts and problems as I do; and stimulation from the exchange of ideas; and I find I question my actions and attitudes far more than before.'

'I am becoming a little more able to distance myself from isolated incidents and able to see how they relate to a child's (or class's) problems. Practice in working out and trying strategies to help situations improve. Feeling that I am not alone in my position.'

'A wider understanding of difficult children. A greater experience of the problem experienced by other teachers. An enlarged repertoire of approaches to try with problem children. A chance to get my own worries off my chest.'

Teachers especially appreciated the atmosphere of supportive interdependence that the meetings established and in follow up sessions were able at times to report 'dramatic improvements' in a child's response at school. While obviously welcoming any positive developments, the consultant was on these occasions at pains to point out the long-term nature of the strategy to help the child and emphasised that there could be no miracle cures. This was a perspective that the teachers came increasingly to share:

'I came in the expectation of instant solutions – having to think things through was a nasty shock at first but now gives increasing satisfaction.'

'These problems cannot be solved in a short space of time.'
(Baker and Sikora, 1982, quoted in Hanko, 1995, p 46)

Following this evaluated project, Hanko has continued to work with authorities and individual schools to encourage the development of similar teacher support groups, an approach further encouraged by the present legal requirement to educate pupils with special educational needs in mainstream schools and classrooms wherever possible, and given the seal of approval in the Elton Report (1989). The coordinator of such a group may be an outside consultant, such as a local authority educational psychologist, or an internal member of staff with the necessary expertise, a role that Hanko sees the SENCO (special educational needs coordinator) increasingly equipped to play. The composition of the group may vary, depending on the needs of the school, but it is recommended that the head teacher is not a permanent member because of the potential evaluative slant that this could place on the group and the inhibiting effect that this might have on individual members. A core of long-term members may provide stability and contin-uity, with other teachers joining on a short-term or ad hoc basis to present and follow through individual cases.

From the point of view of this present book, the following aspects of Hanko's approach are of particular interest:

- the respect given to all participating teachers, irrespective of status and length of experience;
- acknowledgement of the reality to the teacher of the difficulties experi-enced with particular pupils, whatever their source;
- acknowledgement of the validity of teachers' perceptions of the problems as a starting point for discussion;
- creation of an ethos in the groups, in which teachers feel able to acknowl-edge difficulties;
- avoidance of direct 'advice'; trust in the teacher's professionalism to make appropriate use of the insights that arise out of collective discussion;
- the collaborative nature of the analysis and discussion;
- the recognition of the power and potential for distortion of the emotions aroused through pupils' challenging behaviour; the accepting security offered by the groups for a more dispassionate evaluation of the problem;
- the cumulative development of skills of analysis and problem-solving.

The above represent the ideal situation if the groups operate in the way Hanko envisages. Certainly, the evaluation of the original project quoted above indicates that where Hanko, as external consultant, was the coordina-tor of the groups, teachers found them both supportive and developmental. The extract from the evaluation included by Hanko does not contain dissent-ing voices. However, Hanko herself refers to her own analysis of groups that have not succeeded (pp 99–100). She identifies as contributory factors to the failure, any features in the setting up and operation of the groups that imply criticism of the teachers, coercion to attend the meetings, or marginalization of the meetings within the school's priorities. Clearly, the existence of the groups needs to be seen by school management as a pivotal resource in their support structures for teachers. Other research (*cf* Creese, Norwich and Daniels below) and my own fieldwork also highlight the attitudes of senior management to peer support groups as contributing to their success or failure.

There is no information about the success of groups that did not use Hanko as coordinator. Hanko herself stresses the need for careful training of potential coordinators in group dynamics and the sensitive handling of critical incidents in the group's proceedings. The creation and preservation of the secure, non-judgemental ethos within the group would seem to be essential to its successful operation as a support group. Beyond that, I would argue that the same secure and non-judgemental attitude, the same trust in teachers' professionalism, and the same recognition of the difficulties teachers encounter in the classroom, needs to pervade the relationships and interactions in general between colleagues and between management and class teachers, if such groups are to have maximum impact.

Like many other teacher support initiatives that are imported into a school by outside consultants, Hanko's approach is directed at improving the teacher's response to the difficulties of individual pupils. Although she does mention the way in which the group dynamics of the classroom may confirm a child in playing a particular role in the class, there is little sense of the total classroom situation in which the individual teacher is operating. My own experience, and data gathered from fieldwork participants suggests that teachers often know what they should be doing to help individual pupils, but are frustrated by the competing claims of other pupils' needs. Powerlessness, frustration and distorting emotion arise not always from lack of knowledge or skill to meet individual needs, but sometimes from lack of a teaching situation conducive to doing so.

Support groups that mobilize the collective skills of colleagues in devising solutions to individual problems in the short term, and contribute to the further development of professional skills in the longer term, are a welcome component of a school's teacher support structures. But I find myself asking: what support is there for the teacher at the moment of crisis, before she has access to the support group? What support is there as she tries to put into operation the insights gained from the meetings concerning the needs of one individual, while others in the class exhibit their own long-standing or more recent needs? As Hanko stresses, there are no short cuts to lasting solutions. With time, teachers' growing self-confidence and expertise in dealing with challenging behaviour will help to make such behaviour less frequent, but that 'supported' time must be available to them, to allow them to start turning round a 'difficult' pupil, possibly in a 'difficult' class.

My next review concerns another peer support project, which also arose to meet teachers' concerns about pupils' special educational needs in mainstream secondary schools, and which is greatly influenced by Hanko's work.

Creese, Norwich and Daniels – teacher support teams

This research, commissioned by the DfEE, aimed to set up, support and evaluate a structure of peer support in secondary schools. The model used, pioneered in the United States, involved Teacher (or Staff) Support Teams (TSTs or SSTs) consisting of three to five teachers who meet regularly with self-referred colleagues to discuss difficulties with individual pupils or groups of pupils. Creese, Norwich and Daniels (1997b) define a teacher support team as follows: 'A TST is an organized system of peer support which consists of a small group of teachers who take referrals from individual teachers on a voluntary basis. The referring teacher brings concerns about classes, groups or individuals in order to discuss and problem solve with their peers. Follow-up meetings are held as necessary.' It was hoped that TSTs would assist teachers in understanding and carrying out their responsibilities towards pupils with special educational needs in accordance with the Code of Practice. The initiative also aimed to counteract the isolation experienced by class teachers in secondary schools, encouraged by their training and by the culture of schools.

Five secondary schools undertook the training days prior to setting up their TSTs, but one of the five, although interested in principle, was unable to set up a team because of pressing priorities to do with an imminent OFSTED inspection (an interesting comment on schools' perceptions of current priorities). The four schools that did undertake the project represented a range of demographic and organizational features. The project was generally well received by the participating schools and the collaborative experience found valuable both by the support teams and by the referring teachers:

> I think in teaching we are far too isolated. We're so busy thinking about the pupils and everything else that we very rarely think about ourselves. If you think how much it costs to train us and employ us. If you think you've got 32 pupils in a classroom, there's all sorts of reasons that make them work, but if the teacher isn't functioning properly, then automatically children are affected. How much time you spend discussing actually helps teachers do their job better. I think it's an excellent idea [TSTs] and I think there ought to be far more of it. It's very poor how little support in the system teachers get. It's disgraceful.
>
> (Creese, Norwich and Daniels, 1997a, p 27)

In spite of general approval for TSTs in principle, the future for the TST in three of the four schools was uncertain at the end of the research team's involvement. Only in one school could the researchers feel confident that the TST would continue. Creese, Norwich and Daniels identify the factors that may contribute to the continuance or otherwise of the project as follows:

- the priority given to the TST by the senior management team, in terms of institutional status, publicity and protected time for meetings;
- the extent to which the TST becomes integrated within the existing support structures of the school, rather than remaining as a peripheral activity, unconnected with other school systems;
- the extent to which ownership of the TST and its activities is under the control of the teachers themselves, and not perceived as fulfilling management-directed purposes;
- the voluntary participation of both team members and referring teachers;
- clarity about the focus of the TSTs;
- the listening and support skills of the team.

The research method used by the university team evaluating the project was a combination of quantitative (questionnaire) and qualitative (interviews) approaches. However, the sample was very small: four TSTs with a total of 20 referrals between them over four terms. Thus, the indications arising from the questionnaire data can only be regarded as tentative. The interview data yielded some interesting pointers as to how teachers perceived their support needs, and I should have welcomed more direct quotations from the teachers. The experience of referring teachers appears to have been positive in all but two cases; but it would have been valuable to know more about their perceptions of the problems they presented both before and after discussion in the team.

Given the relatively small number of referrals over the four schools, it would also be interesting to know more about the perceptions of non-referring teachers. Their response to the questionnaires showed positive interest in the TSTs, but there is little indication of why they were not used to a greater extent. In one school, the senior management team clearly viewed the TSTs as a medium through which to influence the performance of certain teachers, and those teachers failed to refer themselves. This throws some light, perhaps, on the possible fears or hesitations of non-referring teachers.

More information would also have been valuable about the processes of setting up the TSTs in the first place. How did schools respond initially to the structure, functions and methods of working of the TSTs as presented by the research team? To what extent were the individual school participants able to modify the project to suit their school? And how were these modifications arrived at? To what extent were whole school staffs consulted before and during the process of setting up a TST about the precise form and function it should have in their school? In other words, how much ownership of the project by school staffs was encouraged from the outset both by the research team and by the senior managements of the schools?

As with Hanko's consultative groups, a specific structure of support was introduced to schools by an external agent. Although both types clearly have great value and potential, it would be interesting to explore a peer support group that had arisen within the school in answer to perceived and articulated needs of its teachers. This is partially addressed in my account of Eastbank School's self-help project.

The implications of the above research for this book are as follows:

- Some teachers feel unsupported within existing structures in secondary schools.
- Some teachers feel isolated in dealing with pupils presenting behavioural/ learning difficulties.
- There is considerable support in principle for teacher support groups.
- The TST project is 'teacher-centred': it is based on the belief that supporting teachers is the most effective way of supporting pupils.
- TSTs, like Hanko's project, seek to harness and develop the skills of teachers for the benefit of their peers.
- However, unlike Hanko's approach, which assumes an equality between all members of a consultative group, there is an implicit inequality between the teacher support team and the referring teacher.
- The emphasis in the TST project, as in Hanko's project, is on problem-solving between colleagues; but the structure of TSTs, the membership of the team and the conflicting agendas of participants may make this problematic.
- The success of TSTs may be compromised where senior managements, under pressure themselves from externally imposed legislation and expectations, do not allow the TST the necessary high profile, status and protected time.
- TSTs may also be jeopardized where they are perceived by teachers to have an evaluative and corrective purpose; or where the nature of the problems presented is defined by the team members rather than by the referring teacher.
- The TST seems to function well, according to the research, in a school 1) that already has a high academic profile and below average social and behavioural difficulties, and is therefore under less pressure; 2) that exhibits considerable cohesion between staff and between senior management and staff; 3) that already has effective discipline and support structures, which the TST is perceived to complement; 4) where difficulties with individual pupils or groups are perceived to be a normal part of every teacher's experience, whatever their status, and referral to the team is perceived as a professionally competent way of dealing with the problem; and 5) where team membership is voluntary and representative of a wide range of experience and skill. This suggests that teacher support projects are unlikely to have maximum impact in isolation from the total ethos of the school and the institutional attitudes towards classroom management.

Several approaches to peer support have been examined, ranging from Hanko's consultative problem-solving groups, which may operate within a school or between a group of schools, through Creese, Norwich and Daniels' TSTs, which, although problem-solving, have a more directly advisory function, to the varied projects set up within schools to meet school-identified needs (Chisholm, 1994). All have in common a recognition that teachers face problems with individual pupils, groups or classes that it is inappropriate to expect them to deal with on their own; and that teachers themselves have the professional skills, or can acquire them, to support each other in problem-solving approaches to the problems. Collectively, they suggest that the following issues need to be considered when setting up a peer support group in a specific school:

- Will there be a formal coordinator? Will the group have an external or internal coordinator? If internal, will the coordinator be a member of the senior management team, or drawn from the ranks? Will the coordinator have any training in group management?
- Will it consist of a permanent advisory team, as in the TST model, to which individuals voluntarily refer themselves; or of a fluid team of individuals who choose to meet to discuss their own classroom problems with specific pupils, as in the Hanko model?
- Who will have ownership of the group? Will it have an imposed structure and purpose as in the Hanko and TST models, or will the precise form of the group arise from the needs and priorities of staff as they perceive them, as in the Chisholm model?
- What is its status within the school? What are the attitudes of senior management towards the group? Will it have protected time for meetings?
- How will teachers refer themselves to the group? Will they voluntarily bring problems to the group? Or will they be directed to the group as being in need of support?
- How may confidentiality amongst group members and individuals presenting problems be ensured?
- How may trust be developed within the group; and how may members or referring teachers develop confidence that they are not being stigmatized as teachers with problems?

Eastbank School's self-help group

Eastbank's initiative in peer support arose following an adverse OFSTED inspection, a change in school leadership and the appointment of a staff tutor with senior teacher status to be responsible for the personal and professional development of teachers (see Chapter 6). Classroom discipline continued to be a cause for concern amongst staff. By the time the staff tutor was appointed, the Assertive Discipline System had more or less been dismantled. The focus of attention for tackling behavioural problems had swung back again from collective institutional responsibility to the attitudes and responses of the individual class teacher. Teachers no longer had recourse to a central detention system, or an immediate access remove facility. Teachers again felt on their own, without 'immediate' support:

> It is important to feel that one has immediate backing for discipline strategies. In practice, teachers are now very much on their own.

> The Assertive Discipline System gave support to ordinary teachers, which now they no longer have. Teachers are on their own again.
>
> (Teachers, Wilson, 2001)

To replace the remove facility, there was now an on-site referral unit (see Chapter 3), which catered on a medium-term basis for those pupils who caused serious behavioural difficulties. The inference of all these changes was that, except in the case of extremely difficult pupils who could now be removed from the classroom for several weeks at a time, the reasons for classroom management problems were largely to be found in the teaching and management style of the individual teacher and this should now be the focus of remedial attention. Teachers were again expressing anxiety about admitting to having classroom management problems. Again, amongst some teachers, there was a fear of failure: 'Sometimes you need help, and know you will get the help and support you need, but fear that in asking for help you will be seen as a problem' (teacher, Wilson, 2001).

Function of the self-help group

As an approach to tackling behavioural problems at the level of the classroom, the staff tutor had formed a voluntary group of teachers to explore ways of meeting the needs of 'reluctant learners'. The staff tutor described her attitude to supporting teachers with classroom management problems as 'taking a no blame approach', 'starting from where the teacher is at'. The group was open to any teacher who wished to contribute to its work. It was scheduled to meet once a fortnight after school, provided other meetings did not take priority, and the numbers attending were variable with a small core of regular members. One regular member gives these reasons for belonging to the group: 'To help improve things in the school; the fellowship of other teachers; a chance to talk about common problems; a few hints and ideas' (Wilson, 2001).

When I began to observe the group as part of my fieldwork, it had already been working for a term, and the focus for the group during this, its second term was to compile a booklet of good practice in responding to the needs of difficult-to-teach pupils in order to encourage some consistency across the school. The staff tutor designated the group as a self-help rather than peer support group and her aim was to encourage teachers to move beyond the sharing of bad experiences in the classroom to thinking about ways of modifying their own responses to pupils' behavioural difficulties.

From negative to positive – dealing with differences of opinion

The principle of consistency proved as controversial in the self-help group as it had done in operating the ADS. While some members advocated consistent practice, other teachers found reasons why it could not work:

> There is no consistency in how pupils are handled across the faculties. Previously there was some consistency through the Assertive Discipline System, but there were other problems with it . . .

> There is no consistency anywhere. Pupils are faced with different expectations from lesson to lesson.

> Consistency is difficult to achieve. Individuals have their own personalities and ways of doing things.
>
> (Teachers, Wilson, 2001)

In the meetings I attended, teachers did spend quite a lot of the meeting recounting their own bad experiences. There seemed to be a need to get difficult incidents and the emotions generated out of their system before there was the emotional space to consider constructive strategies. In talking to me privately, individual teachers valued this function of the group highly. They appreciated the atmosphere of trust that the group had generated in which they felt able to talk about their own classroom problems and hear those of others. They described the relief of knowing that others shared the same problems and also had other problems of their own, and it was often helpful to hear how others tackled the problems. They enjoyed the group feeling that developed from the sharing of experience. One teacher 'felt secure in the group, and found it reassuring to know that others had similar difficulties, and that others sometimes had different difficulties' (Wilson, 2001).

It is possible that self-help groups that are intended to have a practical outcome work better together if they are not too narrowly utilitarian in conception, and allow the time and space for the emotional and relational dimensions of the group to express themselves. There were also indications that time is needed for controversial issues to be sufficiently well discussed for the individual views of group members to be properly represented. A significant example of this concerns the controversy about the consistent handling of inappropriate pupil behaviour across the school. In one meeting I attended this was a key issue, and much time was spent in debating whether consistency was either possible or desirable or not. The tone of the meeting was negative, with the emphasis on all the reasons why consistency was unachievable and members defending their right to autonomy.

The discussion appeared to have reached stalemate by the end of the meeting, with much precious time having been spent with no agreement reached. Yet in the following meeting, one member suggested that it was possible to agree on a consistent approach in some crucial areas of teachers' classroom activity, which would still leave room for teachers' own individualism. From then on, group members moved on to suggest ways they could behave consistently. The group's working had shifted from the negative to the positive.

It is possible that groups need to facilitate and accommodate the expression of divergent views. Once individuals feel that their particular perceptions have been listened to and appreciated, they are then ready to listen to and appreciate the views of others and move on to constructive compromise and consensus. The 'fallow time' *between* meetings may be an important period when group members have the opportunity to consider divergent views away from the emotional atmosphere of the meeting and the need to defend their corner.

The function of the group task

Members of the group gained satisfaction from the idea that they were contributing something to the working of the school as a whole in compiling the booklet of good practice. There was also some scepticism about the effect that the booklet might have on general practice within the school. The idea of consistent practice across the school had already raised argument in the meetings, and individual members who talked to me expressed doubts that their booklet would have any official status within the school to counter the tendencies for different faculties and individuals to continue to work as they had always done:

> There needed to be more sense of purpose to the group. The idea of producing some guidelines for consistent practice is good, but I wonder how much power the group would have in persuading the rest of the school to adopt suggestions.

> I don't feel that anything constructive could come out of the group. It had no power or influence within the school. Each department has their own way of doing things which they are reluctant to change.
>
> (Teachers, Wilson, 2001)

Competing priorities

The group meetings were suspended because of the preparations for a second, crucial OFSTED visitation and its aftermath. The head wanted all meetings halted to allow teachers to get back to the business of teaching. As a result, most of the collecting up and compiling of the booklet was done by the staff tutor. The individuals I talked to missed the group after its suspension. They missed the companionship of other teachers.

Because of the group's suspension and for other professional reasons, I was not able to explore the operation of the group as extensively or as thoroughly as I had wanted to. Nevertheless, my limited observations and the conversations with individual members of the group convinced me that there were important issues arising to do with the overt and covert reasons for the group's existence, which would be relevant to all forms of peer support.

Issues raised

The progress and conduct of the group during the time I was involved raises the following general questions pertinent to similar self-help groups:

- What are the functions of the group 1) as intended by the coordinator; 2) as experienced by the participants? Are these functions compatible?
- Does difference in status between coordinator and participants matter?
- How are the group members perceived? Are they perceived as having an important contribution to make to whole school developments, or as having problems in need of remedy?
- What is the status of the group task? Is it perceived as having value for the school as a whole, or is it a vehicle for encouraging group members to think about their own practice?
- What is the status of the group within the school organization? The fact that the meetings had low priority against other meetings and that they were suspended altogether prior to the OFSTED visit suggests that Eastbank's group was very vulnerable to other demands on teachers' time.
- What are the perceptions of other teachers towards participants in a group focusing on issues of classroom management? Participants in Eastbank's group revealed to me that they were afraid other people might see them as 'weak' or as 'failing' because they chose to seek the assistance and support of the group. The core membership of the group was small. How many other teachers may have been put off joining the group because of a feared stigma attached to it?
- How are differences of perception and opinion dealt with within the group? How are tensions resolved? By what processes are consensus reached and decisions made?

It became obvious during my observations and discussions, that, whatever its other purposes, the self-help group was performing an important function for the participants in relieving their sense of isolation, of individual failure and insecurity, and giving them a more positive and constructive view of themselves and their value to the school. These are important goals to strive for. Given that peer support groups appear to have such a positive effect on the morale and commitment of teachers, it seems important that they should command a high status within the total institution and be given protected time, and where there is a tangible outcome of the groups' activities in terms of materials or recommendations, these should be assured of an audience.

From a consideration of the literature on peer support groups and from my own observations of the Eastbank self-help group and discussions with participants, the following general points can be made, which may be of help to any school or group of teachers wanting to set up such a group:

- Peer support groups fulfil an important function in combating teachers' isolation and feelings of powerlessness, particularly in dealing with problems of pupils' behaviour and classroom management.
- There is some evidence (Creese, Norwich and Daniels, 1997a) that these are most effective if they are part of a network of support structures within the school, in an ethos that regards pupils' behaviour as a whole school concern.
- There is evidence that these groups should be conceived as professional problem-solving groups rather than counselling groups (Hanko, 1995). There is a danger in cosy, inward-looking support groups, which merely reinforce the views of participants rather than challenge them and subject them to critical scrutiny with a view to encouraging participants to consider alternative attitudes and strategies (Chisholm, 1994).
- Participants should be regarded as having expert contributions to make to the group from their own experience. They should not be regarded as supplicants for advice and support from others with superior knowledge or status (Hanko, 1995).
- Successful peer support groups have been coordinated from outside or within an individual school (Chisholm, 1994; Hanko, 1995; Creese, Norwich and Daniels, 1997a). There are some indications that groups led by members of the senior management team may be suspected by participants of being hijacked to suit management purposes (Hanko, 1995; Creese, Norwich and Daniels, 1997a). However, Eastbank's self-help group was the initiative of the staff tutor, a member of the senior management team, and was warmly supported by its regular members; and I have also heard anecdotally of cases initiated by senior management that have commanded support and commitment from participants. The important factor would appear to be, not the status of the coordinator but the amount of trust that individual already enjoys amongst staff, and can engender amongst the group members.
- For the necessary trust to develop amongst participants, group meetings need to be allocated sufficient time for sharing experiences, discussing problems and differences of view, and reaching decisions.

- A peer support group is likely to be most effective where the general ethos of the school is such that participants do not feel stigmatized through seeking help from the group. The whole issue of teachers' attitudes towards one another and towards failure to control pupils' behaviour is crucial to the discussion about teacher support, and will be returned to later in the book.
- Peer support groups tend to be more effective when participants volunteer to join or to refer themselves because of difficulties they have themselves identified, rather than if they are recommended to the group because of recognized problems.

Collaborative initiatives

Collaborative initiatives may include team teaching arrangements, paired or group action-research initiatives, mentoring partnerships or any informal arrangement between colleagues to pool skills or knowledge or share responsibility for designated aspects of teaching or managing specific classes. There is a body of literature on all these. For the purposes of this book I will treat them all as aspects of one activity, that is, collaborative working arrangements, and summarize the issues that are relevant to teacher support.

It has already been seen that feelings of isolation, powerlessness, and of being unsupported are rife amongst teachers, and that these are partially combated by involvement in whole school development initiatives and by the deployment of extra adults in class groups where there are a number of pupils who need a great deal of attention. Collaborative initiatives are an extension of these arrangements, where two or more colleagues can work together on a jointly defined problem, contributing to the body of expertise available to the school, and at the same time learning from each other and extending their own skills. Where the collaborative project involves direct working in classrooms or with pupils, colleagues reinforce each other's authority, spread the management and teaching load and contribute to a less stressed classroom ethos. Pupils welcome extra adults in classrooms. They gain speedier attention and a greater sense of security. In addition, pupils have access to role models for successful collaboration.

Difficulties are likely to arise from such arrangements where the professional values and objectives of each participant are incompatible, where the purpose of the collaboration or the problem to be addressed has not been fully defined, where the different roles and tasks of each participant have not been fully thought out and where either partner does not have a sufficient trust in and respect for the skills and expertise of the other.

I give an example below, taken from my own experience, of an attempt at collaboration that promised much but ended badly, as a cautionary tale. An analysis of the mistakes I made provides pointers to the issues that have to be taken into consideration in undertaking collaborative ventures.

Dropped stitches – lessons from a failed collaboration

My research fieldwork was undertaken in two separate periods. I carried out the main investigation over the academic year 1995 to 1996, during which the school underwent an unfavourable OFSTED inspection and was put on special measures. When I undertook the follow up fieldwork in 1998, there had been a change in school leadership and the school again faced a critical OFSTED inspection. As part of my follow up fieldwork I had wished to set up a peer support group as a piece of action research. Because of the appointment of the staff tutor since my first period of fieldwork, and her initiative in setting up the self-help group described above, I did not want to overlap with her work and after a period of uncertainty, undertook instead to explore the self-help group as an example of peer support. My initial participation in the group was with the generous permission and blessing of the staff tutor, who expressed an interest in my research and was anxious to be as helpful as possible.

After I had attended two meetings, there was a misunderstanding between the staff tutor and myself about the nature of my research and she made it clear that my presence at future meetings would not be appropriate. She gave me permission to interview individual members of the group for the purposes of my research. Again, there was a serious communication gap between myself and her, and it became impossible for me to continue my involvement in the school. The details of the misunderstanding need not concern us here. I fully understood her position given the nature of the communication gap between us and her partial awareness of what I had set out to achieve through my research. I undertook an analysis of the relationship difficulties that led to the termination of my fieldwork. The issues that emerged are relevant to collaboration in general, and reveal how vulnerable collaborative initiatives are to emotional and professional pressures on the collaborating partners. I summarize these issues below:

- In collaborative partnerships, there is a need to specify from the start the goals of the partnership, the parameters of it and the relative status and role of each of the participants.
- It is necessary to agree on terminology and the definitions of these terms, since much misunderstanding may arise from different interpretations of the terms used.
- Time must be found at the beginning of a collaboration to discuss the above fully and to explain the intentions of each partner and how each prefers to operate.
- Time must be found during a collaboration for a full discussion of any difficulties that may be arising, and for mutual listening and appreciation of the other's point of view.

- Mutual goodwill and trust is essential to deal with any differences of perspective that arise and to reach either a consensus or an acceptable compromise.
- Mutual sensitivity towards the possible pressures on the other is essential, and towards possible threats to the self-image and sense of purpose of each participant.

These issues are relevant whether the collaboration is between two people or a group; between two people of equal status or between more and less senior staff. They are equally appropriate for a peer support group, colleagues undertaking a joint project, or for the partnership between class teacher and support assistant.

Summary and conclusion

I have shown with reference to the literature, my research fieldwork and my own experience how valuable teachers find forms of support that involve collaborating with colleagues to address problems they have identified or to contribute to whole school developments. I have suggested that the benefits of such collaborative initiatives are not limited to the tangible products. Successful collaboration allows teachers to address the emotional issues that arise from classroom interaction and that too often bedevil relationships with pupils. The experience of sharing feelings and concerns combats teachers' sense of isolation and guilt, and the collective assessment and addressing of problems allows teachers to feel empowered, with a renewed sense of identity.

Several researchers have warned against the cosy complacency that support groups may encourage, where, in an effort to be supportive, members are simply validating and reinforcing inappropriate practice. Peer support groups need to find a mechanism or modus operandi, whereby existing practices and attitudes may be challenged constructively, and divergent views acknowledged and accommodated. I have suggested that the time spent in recounting experience and validating the feelings aroused is not wasted time, but an essential catalyst in the creation of the necessary trust and cohesiveness to confront the issues involved. The quality of the leadership of the group, whether this is a formal or informal position, is crucial in moving a group beyond the stage of empathy to constructive and insightful problem-solving.

I do not wish to underestimate or oversimplify the tensions that a critical support group may generate. It is necessary to balance the need for time and emotional space to allow the generation of trust and goodwill between members – if necessary a 'licking of wounds' and 'mutual stroking' time – with the need to move the group on. However, where the necessary trust and goodwill are present, the potential of the group for collective development and action is great.

I have also shown how collaborative initiatives may fall victim to mis-perceptions and misunderstandings between the collaborating partners. Feelings of competitiveness, defensiveness, lack of confidence, inferiority, superiority can all lead to mistrust and conflict. The potential for this must be recognized and time and attention devoted to creating the kind of atmosphere and working relationships where misunderstandings are less likely to happen, and when they happen can be constructively resolved through discussion and goodwill.

Collaborative initiatives, which require time for proper planning and for the discussion and resolution of points of conflict, are vulnerable, as we have seen, to the claims for priority of all the other pressures and demands on teachers. We may have to rethink our priorities. If talk, discussion, collective support and collaborative problem-solving are as valuable to teachers as they appear to be; if they promise to relieve some of the pressure on teachers that make them act inappropriately in the classroom, and allow them to be the kinds of teachers and people they want to be, and that pupils want them to be, then surely they must be given the same kind of status and recognition as recording and reporting procedures and assessment meetings.

Discussion points

- Are there any arrangements for peer support initiatives amongst teachers in your school? If so, who has instigated such arrangements and who co-ordinates them? What is their function? What is the attitude of manage-ment towards members of peer support groups? How is trust generated amongst members of the group? How are divergent views dealt with? How are decisions reached?
- What status do peer support initiatives have in your school? Do they enjoy protected time?
- What is the status of any tangible recommendations or products originat-ing in a peer support group or collaborative project?
- Are you a member of a collaborative partnership or group? What caused you to join? How do you feel about the group? What for you are the advan-tages and disadvantages of such a collaboration? How might it be improved?

I have suggested that participation in collaborative initiatives is a way of relieving teachers' feelings of isolation and powerlessness, and renewing their sense of professional identity. These emotional functions of peer support and self-help groups are very important. But they also have important poten-tial for constructive professional development. Eastbank's whole school discipline system, for example, revealed curriculum areas and individual classes where there seemed to be particular behavioural or relationship problems. It demonstrated the need for a designated member of staff with the appropriate sensitivity and relationship skills to support teachers who were experiencing particular problems. The appointment of the staff tutor was a response to that need.

In designing and introducing the Assertive Discipline System, Eastbank teachers volunteered hours of their time in discussing problems, examining materials, structuring a system that met their school's needs and evaluating it and amending it. The value to them of collectively focusing on a specific area of concern as a form of professional development must have been great. In the next chapter, therefore, I shall discuss the role of the staff tutor and the function of professional development as forms of teacher support.

6 Personal and professional development

I think when people say, well look, why is this happening, why do children have a problem in this area, why do children have a problem with this member of staff, and when those staff are helped . . . I think it's because they need help, but there's no one in this place who could come and give them the training and the help . . . It's like a can of worms, isn't it.

(Teacher, Wilson, 2001)

Opening the can of worms

The success of Eastbank's Assertive Discipline System depended partly on the computer's potential for giving instant access to trends and statistics. All detentions and referrals to the remove room were logged onto the computer along with the name of the relevant teacher. This ensured that individual pupils' behaviour could be tracked and monitored. Pastoral care staff could easily see in what areas of the curriculum and with what members of staff problems seemed to be occurring for particular pupils, and take steps to remedy the situation. It was through using the system, for instance, that staff became fully aware how many pupils were misbehaving because they could not cope with the work. The computer records also provided facts with which the school could discuss pupils' behaviour with their parents, and, if necessary, refer a pupil to the governors with the possibility of suspension. They created a concrete base for cooperative action between the school and the parents.

The computer records also provided information about particular areas of the curriculum and about particular members of staff where there seemed to be specific problems. This was potentially a highly controversial development. As the teacher quoted above said, it opened up 'a whole can of worms'. When particular teachers were seen to be giving out more detentions than the norm or referring more pupils to the remove room than most of their colleagues, what was going on? What structures were available to investigate the reasons, support the individual teacher, suggest alternative strategies?

As several teachers pointed out, the Assertive Discipline System had shown up the gaps in the school's support systems:

> But now what are we doing? Is there any training going on with staff who are putting 15, 20 kids in detention a day? Is there any training going on? Obviously, we've got to respond to children, but also with the staff, and I don't think we're doing anything with the staff because there are no systems in place to deal with it . . . It's a failure of the support in house. Because those staff were always good teachers, but they [can't] deal with the explosions.
>
> (Teacher, Wilson, 2001)

> The need for a sensitive member of staff to work with teachers who were experiencing difficulties with some groups or individuals was voiced by this teacher: 'You need the right sort of person to make that [the support] useful to staff and to give that to staff, and I think teachers are very judgemental about other teachers, and they don't see both sides . . . they see somebody who's having a problem as weak, and they are not necessarily weak.'
>
> (Wilson, 2001)

Teachers agreed on the need for a designated person or persons with the authority, responsibility and the necessary personal skills for offering teachers support and professional development opportunities in response to specific needs. There were, however, different perceptions about where this support should come from. Some said it was a senior management responsibility, others thought the faculty heads were best placed to respond to the difficulties experienced by their own subject staff.

From whatever source, there was a need for professional help and support, which clearly was not available. It was not just teachers who were experiencing particular difficulties who were conscious of a lack of professional validation and reinforcement. Several teachers mentioned the need for praise and critical feedback, without which they felt they were existing in a vacuum: 'I mean, sometimes I feel like a little lost sheep. You know, I do things and I don't know: right or wrong? Nobody ever says . . . oh, they accept it, but they don't say: oh, we don't like this, or we do like this, so, you know, why not?' (Wilson, 2001).

Again, as we have already seen with pupils, teachers are voicing a deep-seated need for confirmation from other significant human beings that they are doing alright or that they can be helped to improve. How well we can understand the needs of pupils if we look into our own vulnerabilities!

The staff tutor

It is ironic that the role of staff tutor with responsibility for the personal and professional development of the teachers was identified as a need through the Assertive Discipline System, but was not actually created until the system had more or less been dismantled under a new leadership. The staff tutor regarded support as 'every teacher's right'. She defined her role as a 'no blame approach', as 'starting from where the teacher is at', operating from the teacher's present position, not 'from the top down'. There is no doubt, from the unsolicited comments of research participants, that her appointment was welcomed, and her tact and sensitivity greatly appreciated. Teachers were able to trust her discretion and were assured of confidentiality. Since I cannot disguise so unique a role in anonymity, it would be invidious of me to comment in too personal detail on her work. However, conversations with her and with research participants undertaken within the ethical framework of my research allow me to make the following general comments about the role of staff tutor:

- Staff tutors need considerable personal skills in relationship building and in increasing individual morale and confidence.
- They must be able to create trust between themselves and teachers.
- They should not be judgemental, but should endeavour to understand and respond to the needs of teachers as well as pupils.
- They need to tackle the legacy of blame, guilt and shame that accompany difficulties in managing pupils' behaviour.
- The work of the staff tutor must be seen as a key role in the support structures of the school and must therefore command the necessary status and conditions to function effectively. Staff tutors need to be given protected time to work with individuals and/or groups as they feel appropriate and in the way they feel appropriate. They should not be given duties that might conflict with the role of staff tutor, such as staff appraisal.

Staff tutors are unlikely to create the necessary trust between themselves and teachers if they are perceived as being the instruments for manipulating the changes in working practices demanded by senior management or external agencies. They must be perceived by staff as being there to help individual teachers develop their own potential as the teachers they want to be. If staff tutors themselves are under pressure from senior management to produce teachers in a certain mould or to act as undercover agents to monitor and assess teachers' performance, they cannot create the ethos of confidence in which teachers can examine their own work critically and determine their own developmental paths.

Staff tutors who are able to win the trust of teachers are in an ideal position to help teachers deal with the emotions of teaching. As we have seen in earlier chapters, classroom relationships are bedevilled with feelings of conflict, frustration, defensiveness, guilt and insecurity on the part of both teachers and pupils, and much confrontation may be the result of the explosive build up of these emotions. Teachers feel guilty about feelings of rage and aggression, which sometimes find expression in real verbal or physical attacks on pupils and merely compound the destructive feelings of self-accusation and blame. When I discussed this with her, Eastbank's staff tutor acknowledged the reality and strength of the hostile emotions generated in the classroom when hours of effort to create motivating materials are flung back in the teacher's face by rejecting pupils, but reminded me that it is teachers' responsibility to control their own emotions, and recommended the role of external experts in anger management and conflict avoidance.

The staff tutor is in an ideal position to facilitate the training opportunities that meet the needs of teachers as and when they perceive what their own needs are. This does not imply that the staff tutor has to wait passively for individual teachers to acknowledge their own difficulties and ask for help. She or he has the delicate task of supporting teachers and validating their strengths, while helping them to become critically aware of their further developmental needs.

A difficult balancing act

It is a difficult balancing act, ensuring the readiness of teachers who already feel a sense of failure and guilt to benefit from training without them becoming defensive and resistant towards apparently rational solutions to complex, emotionally charged problems. Although, as adults and professionals teachers have the prime responsibility for setting the standards of behaviour and themselves being role models for self-control, it has to be recognized that there are circumstances where the provocation is too great for most teachers to be expected to cope with unaided. Sometimes people have a right to be angry. And given that the expression of anger in physical or verbal violence against the pupil is unacceptable and rarely effective in bringing about a change in behaviour, teachers must have available to them legitimate channels for the expression of that anger. I believe that this need for a safety valve, through which legitimate frustration and anger can find an escape route, is one of the reasons for teachers' need for instant access to remove facilities and to emergency support.

In-service training and professional development opportunities fulfil a dual purpose: to enable teachers to expand and extend their skills and expertise in the directions they choose to move in, to become more nearly the teacher they want to be; and secondly to acquire the skills and expertise that management expects of them to meet government requirements. They are more likely to respond favourably to the latter, if management expectations correspond with teachers' own perceptions of the way in which the profession should move. But this is a wider discussion.

In the next section I look at what some of Eastbank's teachers said about professional development activities as a form of support and suggest the principles that should underline effective in-service training.

In-service training and professional development activities

Comments overheard in the staffroom following an in-service session given by an external consultant on special needs provision in mainstream classes:

> He kept referring to primary schools. I wrote across my paper: 'But we're a secondary school'.

> There was a lot of bore factor.

> It was a good case of teaching your grandmother to suck eggs.
> (Personal research journal, quoted in Wilson, 2001)

I reproduce these comments because they are typical of the kinds of responses to many of the training day activities that go on in schools. In one school I taught at, a group of teachers chatted their way through a presentation by an external consultant, just as though they were alienated adolescents. When asked if they would mind listening, one of them said: 'But I'm not interested.'

Does this mean that teachers are unwilling to step outside their own insularity to learn about new ideas and new approaches? Of course not. Here are some of the suggestions Eastbank teachers made about the kinds of professional development they found valuable: discussion with colleagues, opportunities to share experience, observation of colleagues at work, shared teaching, workshops with colleagues to attend to problems identified by themselves (Wilson, 2001). One teacher had negotiated with a colleague to observe the colleague's handling of a class she herself found difficult to manage. She was also trying to get time out of school to observe teachers in her subject in other schools to learn new approaches.

The important points about all these suggestions are that, firstly, the motivation for undertaking these activities sprang from the teachers' perceptions of their own needs; secondly, the activities involved interaction with colleagues; and thirdly, there was an assumption that teachers are professional enough and competent enough to gain insight into their own needs and to act as consultants and advisers to each other.

I once felt a slight resentment in being directed to an in-service course on positive teaching by a deputy head who had no direct experience of my teaching and no knowledge about how I perceived my training needs. The source of my resentment was his assumptions about the reasons for the difficulties in classroom management I was experiencing at the time. He took it for granted that if I was having difficulties then they must be down to my failures in relationship building, lesson preparation or presentation. In other words, I was being directed to this course because I was seen as weak. Given the amounts of time, energy and thought I gave to my work, and the extent already of my self-criticism and feelings of inadequacy, his apparent assumptions about me only added to my low morale.

I had no objection to the course itself. The principles on which it was based corresponded with what I was trying to achieve. But that was the problem. Theoretical principles, however sound, however rational, have a tendency to get lost in the emotional complexities of the real situation. They tend to interpret the situation from a unidimensional standpoint, in this case: pupils will respond better to praise, encouragement, positive reinforcements of all kinds, rather than to attention being paid to their negative behaviour through shouting, belittlement and various sanctions. As has been seen, pupils' own statements seem to confirm this. But, as has also been seen, other elements of the classroom situation, peer pressure, emotional conflict, teachers' own frustrations and guilt feelings, conspire against the simple equation: positive handling equals cooperative behaviour.

I tell this anecdote because it reflects insights I have discovered through my research about attitudes to in-service training that is imposed rather than freely chosen; and to support, both in the spirit in which support is offered and in the spirit in which it is received.

Self-directed professional development

The entry from my research journal quoted at the head of this section suggests that teachers resent so-called experts coming in from outside to tell them how to conduct their classes without reference to the context of the school or the particularities of individual groups. From their statements about kinds of in-service training they do find valuable it is possible to summarize the factors that contribute to successful forms of professional development:

- Teachers are most likely to accept professional development activities that address problems they themselves have identified.
- They are more likely to benefit from activities that draw on their strengths rather than underline their weaknesses.
- They welcome opportunities to collaborate with others on projects of mutual benefit.
- They welcome opportunities to collaborate on activities that will benefit the whole school.
- They welcome opportunities to observe other teachers either within their own school or in other schools.
- They welcome opportunities to discuss problems with other teachers.

The activities going on in Eastbank School, which I have described as supporting teachers, can also be seen as forms of professional development since they encouraged teachers to look critically at their own practice and question the philosophy that underpinned it. Both the Assertive Discipline and the self-help projects brought teachers together to discuss shared problems and to explore potential solutions. The post-Elton Report project that Eastbank School embarked on as a preliminary enquiry, which finally led to the Assertive Discipline System, involved teachers in undertaking structured observation in colleagues' classrooms. This brought teachers out of their own specialist isolation to appreciate the work of colleagues across the curriculum. As one teacher said, 'I didn't realize how difficult teaching modern languages is.' The initiative led to further discussion about the nature of the behavioural problems teachers encountered across the school and caused them to challenge their own practices.

Further examples of collaboration as professional development

Projects that I myself have been involved in are relevant here as examples of the developmental benefit to be gained from various forms of collaboration.

A departmental project

In one school I taught in, we set up a departmental project to both observe and be observed in each other's classrooms, choosing in advance the particular skill we wished to focus on, and choosing teachers to observe who were known to be strong in that particular skill. One colleague, for example, had developed strategies for conducting his lessons exclusively in the foreign language to a greater extent than the rest of us had managed to do, and he hosted several observation sessions.

A cross-departmental project

I do not wish to imply that external agencies are of no value in promoting professional development activities, but their most effective role is that of coordinator or catalyst in stimulating and evaluating collaborative projects within the school. One school I taught in became involved in a project insti-gated by a team of professionals based at a local university. This was a school-wide project in which foci of relevance across the curriculum were chosen and each department contributed their own ways of fulfilling the pro-ject's objectives. The management of the project used a cascade model whereby representatives from the staff were trained by the project team in the structure of the project. They in turn both communicated with the whole staff and liaised with representatives from each faculty.

Participation in the project generated a lot of enthusiasm. My own personal reservations concerned the imposition of a structure from outside and the hierarchical system of project management. I personally felt a long way from the hub of the project, carrying out tasks decided on by others. Clearly, some form of balance has to be achieved between the benefits to be gained from a whole school developmental project, with much of the administrative planning undertaken by the external agents, and the disadvantages of large-scale projects that may devalue the individual teacher, who may experience the requirements of the project as just one more imposed structure.

A cross-schools project

A further large-scale project in which I was involved some years ago as external coordinator is relevant here as it highlights many of the factors involved in supportive projects highlighted above. At the time I was a field officer for the Centre for Information and Advice on Educational Disadvantage, a national organization whose remit was to explore and disseminate examples of good practice in giving disadvantaged groups better access to education and more opportunities to achieve.

I was involved in a project concerned with language and literacy in 10- to 14-year-old pupils. My role was to coordinate the contributions to this project made by a group of schools in the North East of England. The structure I was given involved each school in the project volunteering a member of staff from their English Department, who would offer an example of their practice for observation and dissemination initially by me as regional coordinator.

However, after my first round of visits to each participating school to observe the practice, the project took off in unpredicted ways, fuelled by the enthusiasm of the participants themselves. The mere fact of being involved in a regional project and having someone from outside take an interest in them and the problems they and their pupils faced, boosted the morale of the participating teachers and motivated them to look more critically at their own work and try to develop it. They began to seek ideas from the other participants in the project. We organized a day conference where they could learn more about some of the most innovative work offered to the project, and exchange views informally with other teachers. As a follow up to this day conference, teachers were invited to some of the schools to observe the projects in action.

Having started from an external project with an imposed structure, it developed a momentum of its own as it was flexible enough to accommodate the needs of teachers as they perceived them. The enduring impressions I took away from this project were the isolation of teachers working in difficult schools and their need for recognition and encouragement; and the desire of teachers for contact with one another, to share with and learn from one another.

Building on strengths

Forms of professional development, therefore, need to be closely related to the needs of teachers as they themselves identify them. Like all the forms of support I have discussed, their acceptability to teachers will depend upon the spirit in which they are offered. Professional development initiatives that are offered as remediation of failure are likely to set up resistances. Initiatives that are offered to maximize strengths and extend the range of skills are more likely to be positively received. Teachers are not, on the whole, self-deluding, obstructionist Luddites. They are committed to doing their job to the very best of their ability. They have a creative need to develop their work and to innovate, provided that the circumstances are favourable. Teachers who already feel overpressured and undervalued, who work long hours in their own time as well as in school to fulfil the demands made upon them, are less likely to want to travel after school to external centres for professional development and take yet more time away from family and relaxation activities.

Other potentially supportive initiatives

Many initiatives to be found in schools have the potential to be supportive to teachers, provided that they are instigated in the spirit of helping teachers in situations where they can legitimately expect support. I end this chapter by discussing another recent development, namely mentoring.

Mentoring systems

In this country, the role of mentor was first introduced in teaching in connection with school-based initial teacher training. In the United States, however, the concept of mentoring has a longer history of workplace support. More recently, in UK schools, it is becoming associated with systems of teacher appraisal and has connotations of monitoring and assessing rather than of support. One head of faculty, for example, was embarrassed about her mentoring role, reluctant to observe in the classrooms of experienced teachers. The tradition of teacher isolation in their own classroom is still so strong in British secondary schools, that mentoring schemes that involve direct classroom observation may well be experienced as threatening by teachers.

Again, like other potentially supportive initiatives, it depends on the spirit in which it is undertaken. Where mentoring is undertaken for purposes of fault-finding and assessment, it may well result in defensiveness and resentment on the part of teachers. Where it is part of an ongoing dialogue between teachers and managers aimed at supporting teachers in realizing their full professional potential, it may be a very useful tool to help teachers articulate their teaching purposes and find the best ways of achieving them. Teachers' reluctance to be observed in the classroom is in fact being gradually eroded as teachers become more used to having others work alongside them: support teachers and assistants, student teachers, researchers. Where senior management and faculty heads have a very visible presence around the school, calling in on classes, prepared to teach alongside the class teacher, the mentoring role becomes an extension of collegiate support.

Teacher-friendly staff appraisal

In one school I taught in, the head teacher introduced a system of staff appraisal ahead of one imposed by the authority. It promised to be a very constructive scheme with considerable potential for staff development and allowing for a great deal of dialogue and participation between the appraiser and appraisee. Its main purpose was to allow the appraisee to articulate strengths and weaknesses and to identify both their own professional development needs and the resources required to meet those needs. The appraisee was offered a list of four potential appraisers, from which their eventual appraiser would be selected. They could accept all of them or reject some of them without having to give reasons. This ensured that their appraiser was somebody with whom they had a good, trusting professional relationship.

When the appraiser was allocated, the appraisee and the appraiser met to discuss a focus for the first round of appraisal. We were advised to select a strength rather than a weakness until we had become confident about the appraisal process. For example, I chose to be observed during the initial lesson of a new topic, because I enjoyed devising motivating ways of introducing the new language. Then there was a lesson observation, focusing on the chosen element. For this I used puppets to simulate dialogues illustrating the new language to be covered. Following the lesson the appraiser met the appraisee to discuss the lesson and draft a report. Aspects of the lesson that might detract from its effectiveness were not ignored (in my case, a group of pupils who were intent on disrupting the lesson), and ways of developing the strategies further were suggested. The final report was included in the teacher's file and a copy given to the appraisee. The whole process emphasized the positive and aimed to be a constructive learning experience. Personally, I found it a very helpful scheme.

Since then, teacher appraisal has become linked with payment differentials and the whole process risks being competitive and judgemental rather than a form of professional development and peer support.

Co-mentoring

In the United States, there has been research into different models of mentoring. Instead of the customary status differential between mentor and mentee (for example, a faculty head and a student teacher; a faculty head and a class teacher), one piece of research (Showers and Joyce, 1996) involved pairs of class teachers of equal status and was a form of mutual peer support. During lesson observations, the usual process was reversed. The observer was learning from the teacher. Each of the mentoring pair acted as critical friend to the other.

Another study (Bainer and Didham, 1994) looked at a range of support and mentoring arrangements in schools, both formal and informal. The authors say that teachers have specific support needs to do with the nature of teaching. Their results imply that a model of support based solely on a mentor–mentee relationship is unlikely to meet all teachers' support needs and suggest that an organizational structure is required that allows for the creation of a range of support relationships to emerge, both formal and informal.

Summary

The initiatives discussed in this chapter, the employment of a staff tutor, professional development, mentoring and appraisal all depend for their success, in terms of supporting teachers, on the trust engendered between the teacher and the organizers of the initiative. Teachers need to be regarded as professionals who can be trusted to take control of their own self-improvement provided that they have the right conditions and resources to do so. They also need to feel that they are not automatically blamed for lessons that go wrong, pupils who do not behave or who do not learn. I have already shown in Part I how vulnerable both teachers and pupils are to frustration and demoralization when the kind of people they want to be cannot be expressed. I suggest that the kinds of support needed are not only the rationally conceived support systems I discussed in Part II, although all these have an important role to play. But real support is likely to be directed at teachers' emotions, at helping teachers to realize the kind of person and professional that they want to be, and can only be achieved through understanding the emotional dynamics of the classroom.

Discussion points

- Does your school employ a staff development tutor? What is her or his status and function? How does she or he orientate her or himself towards management purposes on the one hand and towards the needs of individual teachers on the other?
- What are the arrangements for staff development and in-service training? How much staff development takes place in-house? What arrangements are there for teachers to pursue training and development courses of their own choosing to meet their own needs? How much opportunity is there for teachers to observe other teachers in the school, to engage in shared teaching, to visit other schools?

- Does your school operate a mentoring scheme 1) for student teachers; 2) for qualified teachers? What is the main function of the scheme? Who participates? What are the attitudes of 1) mentors; 2) mentees to the scheme? Can it be made more supportive? Is there protected time for mentors and mentees to meet to discuss issues?
- What kind of appraisal system is operating in your school? Has it been imposed on the school or developed within the school? What is its main function? What are the attitudes of staff to it? Can it be made more supportive of staff?

Conclusion to Parts I and II

My overall objective in writing this book is to contribute to the development of classrooms in which both teachers and pupils can engage in mutually satisfying teaching and learning activities and can interact in a spirit of reciprocal respect. In Part I, I examined the situation in which teachers find themselves from their perspective. I identified what teachers perceive to be some of the barriers to the satisfying practice of their profession and what their classroom needs are. I have described some of the support initiatives put in place at Eastbank School, and teachers' reactions to them.

My argument so far is that because of all the recent changes in education, teachers have been forced to question, relinquish or act against their deeply held philosophies of education. They experience great uncertainty about their current role and about the underlying values and purposes that inform their work and their dealings with pupils. They are deeply insecure in their classroom relationships, and have little leeway in terms of time and emotional space to respond appropriately to pupils' needs. The consequent frustration and stress leads to distorted behaviour on the part of the teacher, which triggers a chain reaction often resulting in outright confrontation with pupils. Teachers' needs, as they define them, are:

- the security of a school-wide discipline structure based on agreed values and procedures;
- management support for their professional judgement and actions;
- more adult help in the classroom;
- provisions that allow them time and emotional space to deal with situations appropriate to everyone's needs;
- a member of staff with the sensitivity and expertise to support teachers in professional development; opportunities for in-service training and professional development based on teachers' own identification of their individual or collective problems and needs;
- appreciation and constructive feedback;
- opportunities for relaxed, informal interaction with colleagues, and for more structured peer support and collaborative projects;

- the feeling of being a valued member of the school, making a valuable contribution to the well-being and development of the school as a whole.

Classroom interaction is, however, a complex interweaving of the needs of both adults and pupils. When things go wrong, it is unlikely to be caused by the inadequacies, misjudgements, needs or frustrations of the teacher alone. In Chapter 2, I examined the classroom situation from the point of view of pupils, based on informal and semi-structured conversations I had with boys and girls in Eastbank School, reinforced by the recorded conversations I had with pupils during my own teaching years. I have shown that pupils also have their needs for security, respect, positive appreciation and personal support from adults, but also for peer approval and status. Just as teachers experience conflict between the kind of teacher they want to be and the kind of teacher they appear to be from their classroom behaviour, pupils also experience conflict between the kind of people they want to show themselves to be to valued adults and the ways in which they are sometimes compelled to behave in the classroom in order to win or maintain credibility with their friends. Classroom interaction often degenerates into a clash of needs.

In Part III, Chapter 7, I suggest a framework for supporting teachers, which incorporates the needs of teachers identified in Parts I and II into a coherent structure that can be used to trigger discussion within schools.

Chapter 8 explores the wider implications of this framework for a philosophy of teaching and learning that is based not on conflict and confrontation, but on dialogue, negotiation, consensus and collaboration.

Part III

The talking school

7 A supportive school

The purpose of support as it emerges from my research is to enable teachers and pupils to behave towards each other with respect and civility, to allow teachers to assist effectively in the intellectual, social and personal development of children and young people, and to provide an ethos in which teachers can operate according to their own personal and professional values and teaching objectives.

It has been seen that teachers tend to view teaching as a humanistic pursuit, intricately involved with human interactions and relationships, and are suspicious of structures and procedures that may become too mechanized and lack the flexibility to incorporate individual perceptions, personal wisdom and specific circumstances. Other researchers (A Hargreaves, 1994; Woods *et al*, 1997) have pointed out that teaching is a creative activity, and that teachers need the freedom to find the most imaginative and appropriate solutions to the classroom problems they encounter, whether these are to do with teaching approaches or management strategies.

It has also been seen that both teachers and pupils may be under such pressure in the classroom situation that they find themselves behaving in ways that are at variance with the kinds of people they want to be, and want others to perceive them to be. Misperceptions of each other may lead to a downward spiral of deteriorating relationships, conflict and confrontation.

Support, therefore, provides an environment in which teachers can remain creative and risk-taking in their approach to teaching, while easing the stresses on both teachers and pupils that may lead to misunderstanding and conflict. It will become evident that support for teachers cannot be considered as a set of add on provisions to cater for teachers who cannot cope, but must spring from a complex of values and attitudes to schooling and teaching that prioritizes human relationships and permeates the school.

The basic proposition that underpins this book is that a school that supports its teachers will inevitably support its pupils, since the overarching aim of the vast majority of teachers is the well-being and wholesome development of children and young people.

A model of teacher support

The model of teacher support that I propose as a starting point for discussion within schools rests on the two principles that 1) the twin objectives of teachers are to communicate knowledge and skills effectively and to facilitate the wholesome development of pupils and 2) the goal of teacher support is to provide an environment in which teachers are able to fulfil these objectives in benign and satisfying ways.

In order to retain their integrity of self, teachers need to reflect in their behaviour both their professional and personal values. Teacher support will therefore be directed at the teacher as a *person* and the teacher as a *professional*. It will operate on three levels:

1 *facilitative*: enabling teachers to be the teachers they want to be;
2 *preventative*: providing safety valves and safety nets;
3 *restitutive*: repairing cracked relationships.

The examples given in the following more detailed description of the three levels of support are illustrative rather than prescriptive. It is in the nature of the model of support I am suggesting that schools themselves embark on whole staff discussion about the values that underpin the school's work, the personal and professional purposes that inform teachers' work within the framework of school values, and the kinds of support that teachers themselves perceive that they need.

Facilitative support

This concerns those organizational structures and underlying philosophy and attitudes that create an ethos in which teachers feel involved, empowered, validated and reinforced as teachers, able to develop and reflect the best of themselves in their teaching. Support will not be considered a prop for failing teachers, but a set of enabling relationships and provisions, to which every teacher has access. I am not claiming that every teacher is always right, never makes mistakes, never finds themselves in difficulties or in conflict with the philosophy of the school. What I am assuming is that teachers are in the main humanistic, committed and deeply concerned about the welfare of pupils. A fundamental goodwill, acceptance and respect between management and staff and between colleagues generates dialogue, trust, negotiation and change.

Teachers' own experiences of the various projects described in this book suggest that the following ingredients are found to be supportive of teachers' identities and work:

• a participatory ethos, in which teachers feel able to contribute to whole school values, processes, decision-making and developments, for example, a whole school discipline system, self-help projects;

- a relational and interactive ethos, in which communication between management and teachers, between colleagues and between staff and pupils is considered a priority; recognition of the value of feedback both positive and constructively critical; provision of time and space to negotiate with classroom support staff, with pupils and parents and with external support agencies;
- opportunities for peer support and collaborative projects;
- time and space to relax, socialize and exchange informal support;
- material provision, facilities and personnel appropriate to the effective teaching of subjects, for example, adequate space and equipment, support personnel – classroom, technical and administrative – appropriate facilities for lesson preparation;
- a whole school behavioural policy and discipline structure, underpinned by a value system that enjoys general support and balancing children's need for consistency with teachers' need for flexibility;
- a senior member of staff with the major responsibility and personal skills to oversee the welfare and personal and professional development of staff within an ethos of trust and empowerment;
- the provision of on-site and external opportunities for in-service training and professional development to meet the needs of staff as they recognize and define them;
- the visibility and involvement of senior staff in the day-to-day life of the school.

Preventative support

The complexity of classroom interactions, and the multiplicity of factors that influence them make it almost inevitable that misperceptions and misunderstandings will sometimes occur. The pressures and tensions in relationships may spring from teachers' own personal situations or professional uncertainties, or from the individual circumstances or group loyalties of pupils. We have seen that both teachers and pupils are stressed when their behaviour causes others to perceive them as someone different from the person they ideally wish to be. Preventative support reflects an acknowledgement that tensions and misunderstandings are an inevitable part of classroom life, which will sometimes move beyond what the teacher alone can cope with. There is a need for 'holding measures', which allow teachers and pupils emotional space and distance to regain control of their own emotions. The following practical measures, which teachers recommend, can be described as preventative support that aims to forestall more serious destruction of relationships:

- instant access remove facilities as a temporary holding place for pupils who are seriously disrupting a specific lesson, being insupportably provocative or who lose control of themselves;

- on-call emergency staff to deal with extreme cases of violent or defiant behaviour, or occasionally to sit with a class while the teacher takes time out to cool off and regain emotional control;
- peer support projects within departments to support teachers within the classroom; to supervise pupils excluded from the lesson for short periods or to supervise the class briefly to allow the class teacher to discuss behaviour with a pupil outside the classroom;
- constructive activities for pupils excluded from a lesson, either to continue work or to reflect on their behaviour prior to negotiating their return to the classroom with the teacher;
- talking time for teachers and pupils to discuss incidents, hear and understand each other's point of view, negotiate a return to the classroom;
- discussion/counselling opportunities for teachers at their instigation, where there is the risk of further deterioration in class relationships.

The most important provision, which underpins all the rest, is an ethos that accepts that human relationships are sometimes conflictual, and regards the above as positive contributions to the maintenance of ordered and collaborative classrooms, not as props for failing teachers.

Restitutive support

There will inevitably be occasions when the above measures are insufficient to prevent real confrontation and conflagration from occurring, and both teachers and pupils will act out of character in ways they will later bitterly regret. There may be verbal or physical aggression on either side. Lack of support at the other two levels will make it more likely that this will happen because teachers feel isolated, frustrated and guilty. One of the negative results of incidents arising from loss of self-control on the part of teacher or pupils is that it produces a set of expectations about each other's reactions, which, if repeated, becomes a pattern of responses that can be difficult to break. Restitutive support consists of measures that are designed to facilitate the restoration of positive relationships, and make such breakdowns of communication and control less likely in future. They operate on a no blame basis, on the principle: this has happened, why did it happen? How can we ensure that it does not happen again? The principle of no blame does not imply no responsibility. It tries to avoid mutual recriminations, but it recognizes that we are all accountable for our own actions and must take responsibility for redressing the damage caused when relationships break down. I suggest that the following may be regarded as examples of restitutive support:

- discussion/counselling opportunities for pupils, who are often as shocked as teachers when the emotional explosions occur;

- discussion/counselling opportunities for teachers, who are usually full of guilt and remorse, feelings of failure and worthlessness;
- time for teacher and individual pupils or class group to discuss incidents together, to repair relationships and negotiate a new beginning;
- a plan of action to minimize the chances of such incidents happening again, including possible in-service training opportunities if appropriate.

Personal and professional support

One of the main aims of schooling is to contribute to the personal and social development of children and young people; to help them learn to respect the needs and the personhood of others, and to communicate their own needs and feelings in non-aggressive, non-threatening ways. One of the most potent ways for children to learn is through absorbing the behaviour of the adults they are regularly in contact with. Although I have stated above that restitutive support is founded on mutual responsibility rather than mutual recrimination, the greater responsibility for the tone of interactions in the classroom has to be the adult's. After all, this is the role of an adult and a teacher: to provide the model for acceptable behaviour. For a teacher to behave in less than exemplary ways is human but it is not mature. And teachers need whenever possible to be seen by the young as mature, adult human beings.

As has been seen from Part I, teachers' professional purposes are closely linked to their personal value systems, and professional behaviour that is alien to the kind of person they wish to be is a source of great stress and demoralization, and deeply destructive of the personal and professional self-image. Schools as institutions, therefore, must have at the forefront of their objectives the protection of the maturity and self-respect of its teachers through its provisions for personal and professional support.

However, in line with the obligation on us all for personal accountability, it is incumbent on teachers to follow lifestyles and make professional choices that are likely to maximize rather than diminish their effectiveness as teachers. In my own case, for a number of reasons, I returned to secondary school teaching without retraining, after many years working in other areas of education. I chose to teach in a school that involved 150 miles car travel daily because I identified strongly with the ethos of the school. I fortified myself with strong coffee and tea. I was idealistic about my teaching objectives and overconscientious, and I spent breaks and lunch hours preparing materials, marking work, doing administrative tasks or following up pupils, instead of relaxing in the staffroom and building up my informal support networks. I spent most evenings working and my own social life and personal interests suffered. As my relationships with some individual pupils and groups deteriorated, I became ashamed and deeply demoralized, and I isolated myself even more completely from my colleagues. I had embarked on a vicious downward spiral of failure, alienation and near breakdown.

I tell this cautionary tale as a warning against putting all one's personal eggs into one professional basket. Our first duty as teachers is to ourselves, to keep ourselves physically and mentally as healthy and resilient as possible, to remain fully rounded human beings, to be open to stimulus and personal growth from outside as well as within the profession. Whatever is within our own power to control as far as our physical and mental well-being is concerned, is our own responsibility. We need to eat a balanced diet, sleep adequately, take proper exercise and find space to relax during the working day as well as outside school.

However, if it is our personal responsibility to take care of ourselves within the limits of our control, it is the institutional responsibility of the school to provide the conditions within which teachers can cherish themselves as human beings. The evidence suggests that schools are becoming less rather than more teacher friendly, and the demands on teachers' time outside the classroom are increasing to the point where their health, personal and social lives and sense of well-being are seriously affected (Carlyle and Woods, 2002).

The metaphor of the superteacher

Two of the teachers in my research independently used the term 'super-teacher' to convey their belief that teachers are increasingly and routinely being expected to operate at levels of competence that only the most gifted teachers can hope to reach. This failure to live up to standards imposed on them was experienced as demoralizing. Expectations, said one teacher, should be targeted at what could reasonably be demanded of the majority of teachers. Other teachers expressed this sense of impossible professional demands in terms of what it was doing to their personal lives, and several were contemplating taking early retirement. Two younger teachers talked of withholding commitment to the profession beyond the point where they felt they could cope, even though this involved neglecting responsibilities which, from a professional point of view, they would want to fulfil. It is an ironic result of current attempts to improve teacher quality that they are alienating some of the most committed and conscientious teachers in the profession. Amongst the teachers I interviewed during my research were many who freely admitted to having difficulties sometimes with individuals or groups of pupils. But they also expressed a deep professional commitment to their pupils, and a desire to develop their own performance. Surely, these are the very teachers the system should be nurturing and supporting, not alienating.

Supporting the emotions of teaching

In-service and professional development courses based on rational solutions to carefully analysed problems have their place in schools, of course. Most teachers benefit from exposure to recent thinking about the processes of teaching, or to the latest developments in their own subject, provided that they can see the relevance of such courses to their own teaching situation. Unfortunately, initiatives suggested in in-service courses may appear to fail, because they do not address the emotional climate in the classroom. I can try any number of exciting new approaches to teaching German, but if my relationships with the group are already difficult, the approaches are unlikely to succeed, indeed may even sour relationships all the more, because each new initiative tried and failed increases my frustration and levels of stress.

There is currently a shortage of institutional support initiatives that are targeted on helping teachers to become more emotionally literate; to recognize when their emotions are becoming too aroused and threatening to distort their reactions; to be able to take timely measures to distance their emotions and maintain control over their actions. Some local authorities and schools are providing advice on conflict resolution, de-escalation tactics and anger control, and these are worth exploring. For individual teachers wishing to explore these issues further, the work of Goleman (1995, 1998), Sharp (2001), and Faupel, Herrick and Sharp (1998) may prove valuable.

However, it is not just the emotions produced in the classroom that dictate our responses. In a situation where teachers and young people are interacting at close quarters for several hours a day, with little respite from each other, emotions normally quite unconnected with the teaching situation may be involved on both sides. The experience of bereavement, family break up, domestic conflict or violence, or sexual abuse may colour the emotional responses of teachers and pupils alike. Expert counselling is theoretically available for children and young people, either in school or through external agencies, and teachers should be aware of these and how to access them (Blandford, 1998). The provision of counselling for teachers is worthy of some discussion.

Personal and professional counselling for teachers

Individual teachers obviously have the right to approach social services or counselling agencies on their own behalf, if that is what they feel appropriate to their needs. Some local education authorities are offering stress counselling to teachers. My response to this is ambivalent. I would ask the question, what is the assumption on which the provision of counselling is based? Is the assumption that individual teachers are inevitably to blame for their own high stress levels and inability to cope? Or is there a recognition that factors within the working environment over which the institution has control are also implicated in teacher stress and need to be addressed? The provision of opportunities through a suitably trained staff tutor, or perhaps through group discussion with an external coordinator to identify the sources of emotions and determine ways of taking back control, is a potentially useful ingredient in a supportive structure. The important consideration is that any measures individual teachers embark upon to deal with their current difficulties should be freely chosen by them as offering the potential for help.

The opportunity to discuss in a non-threatening environment incidents where teachers have responded inappropriately is of great importance to the future welfare of the teacher. Entries in my own professional diaries describe the increased sense of isolation and failure I felt on those occasions when I was refused the opportunity to discuss and analyse the situation in order to work through to a more objective appreciation of what was going on and how to respond in future. Personal sympathy from colleagues, though welcome, is not always sufficient. One needs to be helped to distance oneself from the emotions of the situation.

Vulnerable teachers

There are times in teachers' professional lives when they are particularly prone to stress arising from uncertainty about their role. These critical points have been recognized and documented as requiring specific support provision, but this is often found to be inadequate. Student teachers and newly qualified teachers are an obvious example, but even here, although support has improved greatly in recent years, it is sometimes found to be patchy. Teachers returning to the profession after a long absence do not always receive the support they need; and teachers moving from one school to another sometimes are not given the necessary information to help them adjust to new structures and systems, according to one of my informants, herself new to the school. Teachers who are facing redeployment or redundancy because of local authority reorganization schemes are a special case, and outside the remit of this book.

Most of these specific needs can be met within a school ethos that sets the well-being of its teachers as a priority and that encourages the development of trust between individuals. Where communication between management and staff is encouraged and teachers are routinely consulted and listened to, and where the professional development of teachers is one of the concerns of the organization, individual teachers' needs are less likely to be overlooked.

The talking school

There are obviously resource implications in much of what I have written. My argument focuses on the need for an ethos in schools that prioritizes teachers and that creates an atmosphere in which teachers can remain relaxed, outgoing and sensitive to the needs of others, while also maintaining an open and receptive stance to new ideas and processes that may enhance their own performance.

People, time and emotional space

The support structure I have described above depends upon the availability of people, time and emotional space. More teachers are needed, certainly, but they need to be deployed in imaginative ways where they are most needed. It is significant that only a tiny minority of Eastbank's teachers involved in the research mentioned routinely smaller classes as a method of supporting teachers. It was the presence of extra adults in the classes that seemed to offer most support. It may have been that teachers could not see the likelihood in the foreseeable future of substantial reductions in class size. One mentioned smaller classes as a means of supporting teachers but then laughed it off as unrealistic; another said that smaller groups would enable her to give more attention to pupils with special needs, but added that primary schools had the greater need in this respect. I am sure that given the possibility of cutting all classes by half, teachers would jump at the chance, but reducing class size by just a few pupils may be unlikely on its own to make much difference to the amount of attention teachers can give each pupil, particularly in groups where there are significant numbers of pupils needing a lot of help for academic or behavioural reasons.

Extra adults, in a supportive role, including teachers but not exclusively, who can be deployed where there is most need may be a more realistic and ultimately a more creative solution to the problem of how best to give appropriate attention to all pupils. Schools need more teachers, but they also need more adults in many different roles and it would be unfortunate to reduce the discussion about the role of adults in schools and their relationship with pupils to an either/or argument about the relative merits of teachers and classroom support assistants.

To a large extent the availability of time and emotional space depends on the presence of more adults. Teachers not only need non-contact time for preparation, marking and all the administrative tasks they have to do, but they also need time within the class for a considered, imaginative response to the challenges posed, rather than the emotional reaction to the frustration that arises out of having too many things to attend to at once, as the pupil said, 'too much stuff going on'.

Emotional space is the state of mind created when we are not being pressured by external demands or our own emotional reactions to behave in ways that are not appropriate to the situation; or when we have the opportunity to step back from a situation that has provoked excessive emotional arousal and allow ourselves to simmer down and look at things more dispassionately and from the point of view of others besides ourselves. I believe opportunities to maintain or regain emotional space are essential in teaching where teachers are constantly being challenged, often in a manner that attacks their self-image in very personal and fundamental ways.

Time to talk

Underpinning the function of people, time and emotional space within the school structure is the need to create an ethos where benign, constructive and creative human interactions can occur. Talk is a fundamental human activity, and needs to be exploited to the full in a setting in which the young of the species are being nurtured into becoming mature adults. Listening, talking, discussing, appreciating other points of view, negotiating, compromising and collaborating are the skills that are essential to constructive social engagement. These behaviours need to be modelled for the young to encourage them to develop them in themselves.

Teachers should be talking with each other, to support staff, to management, to junior staff, to pupils, to parents, to governors and to support agencies. Time to talk is essential time that should be allowed for in the way the work in schools is structured. Time for talk cannot always be allocated within a formal timetable. We do not always know in advance when situations arise that require talking about. The whole ethos of the school must be flexible enough to accommodate the unpredictable. When children in my class are being uncooperative, I need someone to keep an eye on the class while I take time to talk with the pupils concerned away from the peer group. I should not have to constantly choose between spending my lunch hour preparing materials, relaxing with colleagues, or following up incidents with pupils. The way my work is structured should allow me to do all these things, because all are essential to the complete and satisfying fulfilment of my role. Schooling should be slower-paced for teachers and for pupils.

Forty years ago, at a parents' evening at the first school I taught in, the mother of a pupil in my class, a girl of 11, informed me proudly of all the activities her daughter was giving up to devote more time to her school work. I was depressed even then at the shackles of achievement we were imposing on the lives of children. The attainment- and assessment-led ethos of schools has arguably increased greatly since my childhood (Woods *et al*, 1997). It is perhaps time to consider again what our teaching purposes are.

I am aware that much of this chapter might seem like pie in the sky to those whose responsibility it is to administer and fund our schools. Extra personnel cost money. Time and emotional space are difficult commodities to allow for and account for, when one's remit is to provide tangible evidence of value for money in terms of pupil attendance and achievement levels. My argument is that these characteristics, less obviously justifiable in economic terms, are the qualities in the school that both teachers and pupils are saying they need. Both teachers and pupils are asking for the provisions in school that will allow them to interact in humanistic, constructive and collaborative ways, and in the end these may be the very factors that increase the productivity, job satisfaction and cost-effectiveness of the institution.

8 Conflict or collaboration

Educating for the 21st century

Both the research on which this book is based and the writing of the book emanate from a personal philosophy of education that I shall attempt in this chapter to make more explicit. I believe that the task of helping children and young people to become fully mature, collaborative, creative and fulfilled members of the human race is one of the most fundamental and crucial roles of the adult. Education is non-reducible to subject teaching or skills training. It is concerned with the whole, developing person. If education is a core activity of human societies, then those institutions that play a formal role in educating the young on society's behalf must be given the most favourable conditions judged necessary to do the job effectively.

In this chapter, therefore, I shall argue for a view of education that seeks to develop and practise those qualities and attributes that make us fully human: for example, rationality, empathy, communication skills, toleration of difference, creativity and collaboration. I believe that in a world that seems to be riddled with conflict, schools as organizations can begin to model ways of interacting with one another that are based on trust, negotiation and consensus. So I shall attempt to fashion from the themes that have permeated this book an image of a school that becomes a metaphor for a more humanistic society. I shall talk about the collaborative school, the talking school and finally the humanistic school. But first I have to deal with the issue of conflict.

The conflict model of schools

Consider the following scenario. I am left in charge of a registration class of year eleven pupils, most of whom I do not know. A group of about six large boys are congregated by the door waiting for the bell to sound the end of registration. I do not know whether they are usually allowed to remain out of their seats and do not wish to invite confrontation by demanding something that is not usually expected of them. I try to take the register. I receive what are clearly inaccurate answers designed to wind me up. I ask politely for cooperation, and when I do not get it, I begin to explain, still reasonably, that the register is a legal document, which I am required by law to complete accurately. This is greeted with loud derision from the group by the door. I say, still patiently, 'No, please, just listen.' 'Why should we?' said one of them, whom I will call Craig. 'It isn't interesting.' His manner is mocking and I feel challenged. 'Will you please go out', I say. 'No, why should I?' retorts Craig, defiantly. I finally lose patience. I march over to him, grab him by the collar of his leather jacket and try to propel him through the door. He resists, and I hear the collar tear. 'Now you're for it', he says triumphantly, amidst the delighted laughter of his mates.

What are the dynamics of this incident? It is a tale of two self-images. I had come to the school with idealistic intentions of managing pupils through reasonable expectations, respect and good relationships. Transgressions would be met with discussion and, failing that, with sanctions that fitted the crime, that is, which would make reparation for any negative effects of the misdemeanour. I had already encountered situations where this approach did not work, and where I was faced with serious disruption, so that my confidence in my chosen strategies had taken a serious knock. And yet my self-image, the kind of teacher I wanted to be, depended on making these strategies work. I may well have viewed the large lads by the door with some trepidation and uncertainty, which transmitted itself to the class.

The group by the door obviously considered themselves a sub-group of the class and asserted their identity by separating themselves from the rest. Positioned as they were by the door, they were clearly signalling a degree of disdain for the norms of the class. Craig apparently enjoyed high status within the group or was making a bid for high status, since he initiated and conducted the defiance with the group as appreciative audience. We were playing to completely different rules. Once engaged in doing battle with me, his self-image depended on getting the better of me. My nervousness, probably communicated through non-verbal signals rather than through anything I said, cast me in the role of victim, and aroused the hunting instincts of the boys. In spite of my belief in non-aggressive means of managing classes, I was also part of the tradition that saw inability to control pupils as a sign of weakness and incompetence. I was torn between two conflicting motives: to maintain my reasonable stance or to try to enforce my will over his. In the face of threat the organism responds with flight or fight. I could not withdraw my request for cooperation without losing face and risking further blatant defiance. Feeling completely powerless, I panicked and went on the offensive. In the end, I lost because, as the teacher, I was the one who had the responsibility to keep my self-control.

How else might I have acted? Some would say I should have asserted my authority from the start by asking the group to sit down and threatening action (such as detention) if they refused. This may have worked or it may have provoked an even earlier confrontation. Two different perceptions operated here. It was a registration session, not a lesson. I did not consider standing by the door a serious enough transgression to warrant risking a confrontation, if the boys were not actually disrupting proceedings. They obviously interpreted my non-response as a signal that they could do as they pleased. There is a fundamental dilemma here. I have to give up my attempts to be reasonable to enter a battle of wills not of my choosing. I have to play by their rules, not mine. And I have to engage in this conflict until they decide to give up and I am the winner. I am being forced by young people to be someone I don't want to be.

There are other things I might have done. I might have shrugged off their initial attempts to sabotage the register with humour ('Oh, be like that, then') and enlisted the help of the one or two pupils I knew in the class to fill in the register. Whether I could have got their cooperation depended on the power Craig's group asserted over the rest of the class – an unknown factor. I might have responded to Craig's defiance and insolence by sending another pupil for a senior member of staff, but the ethos of the school at that time was that teachers sorted their own problems and it seemed such a trivial matter to warrant involving senior staff. There was no whole school behavioural system or on-call rota of staff. I felt powerless and isolated, and these feelings must have contributed to my panic reaction.

I have described and analysed this episode in detail because it illustrates well how complex seemingly trivial situations can be, and how easily they can escalate into real confrontations. There are so many factors one needs to take account of in the split second one has to choose a response. And the emotions at work often make a rational response difficult, particularly if one's self-concept is involved. One's survival on a psychological level is threatened as surely as though one were being attacked physically. I needed the support of a system that provided me with somewhere to send Craig if he persisted in his disruption until I could talk to him later. If he refused to go, I needed to be able to send for a senior member of staff to deal with him.

Much of this book has been about conflict situations. One theory of schooling has seen schools as reflecting in microcosm the divisions that go on in the wider society: the conflict between those who have power and those who do not; between different interest groups; between different value systems; between different interpretations of a situation and between different personal needs. In the scenario I have just described, these points of conflict are easy to detect. Craig was part of a sub-group who were in conflict with the accepted norms of the class, and who needed to assert themselves against the teacher as representative of the institutional authority. There was a clash of values between my attempts to reason with him, and his need to exert power. There were two opposed interpretations of the situation: my desire not to invite confrontation being perceived by him as unwillingness to exert my authority. Finally there was a battle of self-images: Craig's need to act hard to retain his status; my need to prove myself as the kind of teacher I wanted to be.

Two models of discipline

Underlying this episode there is a more fundamental conflict between two models of discipline. On the one hand the conflict model described above sees battle between the teacher and pupils as inevitable, and long-term discipline of the group depends on the teacher winning the initial battles. On the other hand, there is the model that relies on reasonable expectations, consistently promoted and reinforced through discussion and encouragement, what I might term the humanistic approach. The difficulty for the teacher is that applying the humanistic approach within an ethos where the conflict approach is expected by the pupils and practised by many of the staff, invites the reputation of being a weak disciplinarian with whom pupils can create a little fun for themselves at the teacher's expense. Teachers who favour a humanistic approach to managing pupils need that approach validated and reinforced by a system that provides the necessary back up facilities.

Reason and emotion

The incident described illustrates well how rational, humanistic intentions can be sabotaged by natural human emotions. The protection of the self: how one views oneself and how others view one is a universal motive after the satisfaction of physical survival needs. Both Craig and I had self-concepts to protect. The confrontation arose because in this situation the factors that would satisfy each of our self-concepts were in direct conflict with each other. I saw myself as reasonable in my expectations and way of handling the situation; he needed to see himself and be seen as a rebel. There was no way in which we were going to find common ground in that arena, with an audience. The negotiations would have to be done elsewhere. This is the dilemma for the humanistic teacher. Given an impossible situation, reason gives way to frustration and emotion and the fight or flight mechanism kicks in.

I was brought up in a humanistic tradition, which sees human reason as our highest quality and the emotions as treacherous hijackers of rational approaches to problems. However, I no longer hold such a dualistic view of human nature. Our emotions, positive and negative, are part of who we are. My desire to help children and young people to develop and learn, and my feelings of satisfaction when I can see that happening are valid ingredients in my motivation to be a teacher. But my anger at being treated with disrespect and insolence as a human being when I do not feel that I deserve such treatment is also a valid human reaction. Our task is to find ways of expressing emotions that are constructive and not destructive to a situation. I needed to find ways of communicating to Craig that his behaviour towards me was unacceptable without becoming involved in the same kind of aggressive, unacceptable behaviour. And I needed to be able to do this before my own emotions became too entangled in the situation.

Unfortunately, the pressures teachers are under from all kinds of sources increase the risk that they will be less able to control their own frustrations and feelings in the classroom. Children and young people also are arguably experiencing increased pressures both from family and social conditions and from the current focus on test results and achievement. Classrooms are potentially explosive places. An essential ingredient in a school's support system both for pupils and for teachers is the recognition of the part emotions play in classroom interaction and the provision of channels where emotions that threaten to become negative can be successfully channelled or diffused. Throughout the book, I have stressed the need for time and emotional space; for holding facilities where pupils presenting difficulties that threaten the activities of the class can be constructively looked after until the problem can be dealt with; for extra staff who can absorb some of the pressures; for counselling, mediation and professional development opportunities to help teachers and pupils to manage their emotions. All these provisions contribute to an ethos that encourages rational and humanistic approaches to managing conflict and guiding pupils' behaviour rather than the conflictual model of discipline that still tends to prevail.

Conflict or collaboration?

Sociological models of schools and classrooms have tended to see conflict as the key concept that illuminates what is going on. The folklore of teachers has also traditionally viewed classroom management as a battle for survival they have to win at all costs. I have shown that there is indeed much conflict to be found in classroom interaction, but is this what we really want? Is this the best we can do for children and young people, 'to keep having to beat them down'?

My research revealed that neither teachers nor pupils want the conflict. Both yearn for classrooms to be civilized places where people are nice to one another, and teachers are there to help pupils learn to make the most of themselves and their lives. Perhaps the very models we have used to explain classroom relationships have ensured the continuation of conflict. If we go into a classroom expecting trouble, our stance, our facial expressions, our tone of voice, our battle-preparedness invite counterattack. I have always found it difficult to relate to the folk wisdom of teachers, advising new recruits 'not to smile till Christmas', and 'to start off hard and ease up later'. Why did I have to be a humourless dictator to earn respect?

Perhaps it is time to look at new models, use a different vocabulary to describe classroom relationships. I want classrooms where teachers are able to express the best of themselves through their teaching and where pupils are able to develop the best of themselves. I want classrooms where relationships between adults and young people are mutually respectful and courteous, where adults can practise tolerance and understanding, sensitivity and empathy, and encourage these qualities in young people. I want classrooms where the differences of purpose, opinion and perspective that arise may be resolved through discussion, negotiation and compromise. In short, I want a model of classrooms built on collaboration and humanistic principles. What are the elements of such a model?

The collaborative classroom

Collaborative classrooms are constructed around the following concepts:

- authority;
- security;
- responsibility;
- communication;
- mutual respect;
- participation;
- common purposes;
- trust.

Authority

This is not to be confused with authoritarianism. Authority is invested in the teacher by virtue of being an adult in a position of responsibility for the welfare and development of children and young people. It is also derived from the teacher's role in communicating knowledge and skills to the young, which society deems essential for adult life, or which the young individual feels to be worthwhile. Authority involves modelling the values the school has chosen to be identified by. And finally, authority resides in the teacher as a person as well as a professional.

Teachers should be able to expect that the institution will back up their authority. Pupils need to feel that authority is not arbitrary, but is based on rational, humanistic principles, which are made explicit to them, and which are there to help them. Teachers need to remain critical towards the bases of their own authority. As children mature towards adulthood, it is to be expected that their attitude to authority will become more critical. They need help in learning how to express criticism in non-antagonistic ways.

Security

Teachers need the security of knowing that they will be supported in being the kind of teacher they aspire to be, and that their authority, values and expectations will be validated and reinforced by the system. They need to feel part of a team with common purposes. Pupils need the security of knowing that there is a system of values that guides their behaviour with the teacher and with each other, and that also guides the behaviour of teachers towards them. Each needs to feel trusted and appreciated, and that their self-image remains unthreatened.

Responsibility

If both teachers and pupils have the right to expect support and security, they also have responsibilities. In their adult and professional role, teachers have the ultimate responsibility for the welfare and development of children and young people while in their care. When relationships break down or the teacher behaves unthinkingly or insensitively, it is a measure of the teacher's maturity to admit accountability and make reparation. But it is also part of the teacher's role to encourage pupils to take responsibility for their own decisions and behaviour, increasingly as they get older, and to become accountable for the results of their own actions. Holding the balance between giving pupils the security of externally determined control, and encouraging responsibility and self-control is a difficult tightrope to walk.

Communication

Just as the friction between parents and children is easier to manage when the channels of communication remain open, teachers and pupils who can talk with each other are likely to have fewer long-lasting breakdowns in relationships. But talking and listening must be a two-way process. How often do we hear pupils say in frustration, 'But you're not listening to me'? And how often do we say, 'Now just calm down and listen for a moment'? When we are emotionally aroused, it is difficult to listen to others. As teachers we tend to talk at children to get our point across; and children will talk back indignantly in an effort to put forward their point of view. We need the right place and time for talking, and this is unlikely to be in front of the class group as audience, nor even outside the classroom immediately after an incident while both teacher and pupil are still emotionally upset. A cooling off time may be necessary for pupil or teacher or both.

Communication is more than the resolution of conflictual situations. A classroom where issues are routinely discussed with pupils, and where values and behavioural expectations are made explicit, allows pupils to feel involved and creates an ethos in which talk rather than force becomes the natural way of dealing with differences.

Discussion is not restricted to behavioural matters. The more pupils are involved in talking about subject content, choosing projects and setting their own targets, the more participatory they feel, and the more ownership they take of their learning. Teamwork, group projects and peer teaching and learning are all means of encouraging collaboration. The ways in which teachers and support staff communicate and collaborate with each other provides pupils with models of reciprocal support.

Mutual respect

Implicit in all that I have written is the concept of mutual respect. Teachers complain that children no longer show any respect for authority; children complain that teachers do not talk to them or treat them with respect. Respect for one another will be at the heart of a collaborative classroom. It is implicit in listening to others and trying to understand their point of view, in consulting others' opinions, in showing consideration for somebody else's feelings, in taking care of other people's property, in accepting and appreciating people for what they are.

Participation

Children and young people, like teachers, want to feel that they are contributing to the good of the class or school. Appropriate to their age and developmental level, they want to be involved in their own learning. They have a greater stake in their progress if they have contributed to decisions about subject content and projects. They want to know why they are studying a particular subject or topic, of what use it will be to them. If educationists or governments believe strongly that certain subjects are essential for an educated adult, they must make a convincing case out to the young people who have to study them.

Common purposes

A collaborative classroom is more likely to succeed where teachers and pupils are in agreement about the learning and behavioural goals of the class. This is most likely to come about where teachers have been able to take the time to discuss these with the class and explain them in the first place, and to keep making them explicit. Common purposes apply to all who work in the class, including support teachers and assistants.

Trust

If the ultimate aim of all the characteristics discussed is the creation of a harmonious learning atmosphere, its attendant result is the generation of trust, without which collaboration cannot be achieved. Above all, whatever the disagreements, the conflicts, the breakdown in communications, pupils need to know that the teacher is ultimately on their side. Where trust has been created, even serious misunderstandings and inappropriate behaviour can be discussed, worked through and forgiven.

This may all read like virtual reality to a teacher struggling as I sometimes struggled with classes where nothing seemed to work. I understand. But when I read the diaries I wrote while I was teaching I was surprised by the indications that I had recorded that I was getting through to pupils in my own way much more than I had realized at the time. But it was such hard, often dispiriting work and in the end I lost confidence in ever being able to work with pupils in the way I wanted to. Teachers who want to manage classes in humanistic rather than conflictual ways cannot achieve it without institutional support.

Nothing I have written should imply that conflict can be eliminated. It is how conflict is dealt with that makes the difference between a conflictual and a collaborative ethos. Children and young people need to learn that some conflict is inevitable, but that it can be resolved without lasting harm to relationships. There will always be differences in perceptions and opinions, competing group interests, power struggles. Where there is a will to manage human relationships and interactions in a civilized fashion, ways can surely be found to negotiate solutions to conflict that respect the needs of individuals. Schools need to model these non-confrontational ways of dealing with difference.

I have demonstrated during the course of the book that much of pupils' bad behaviour in classrooms originates in their need to maintain status with their peer group. This does not only apply to anti-school sub-groups. Even pupils who are in general reasonably conforming are under considerable pressure not to appear too hard-working or high-achieving. I described young people I taught who were pleasant, helpful and cooperative when interacting with me on a one-to-one basis – even in a detention situation. But once back in the classroom they have to do their share of disrupting in order to keep face with their peers. Many pupils want to conform but dare not conform. This is a very difficult situation for teachers to cope with.

One of the fundamental needs of human beings is group membership and the sense of identity this confers. We have to acknowledge the importance to pupils of their friendship groups, whilst encouraging them to develop the judgement and the strength of character to resist those group values that are against their own interests. For pupils who feel they are failing in those activities the school values, membership of an anti-school group becomes their only way of asserting themselves and retaining a sense of identity. Pupils need the opportunity to belong to a wide range of interest groups and to have many avenues to achievement, if they are not to over-identify with a single group. In the present educational ethos of narrow educational objectives, achievement targets, assessment and league tables, there is a danger that lower achieving pupils will become more not less alienated from the values of school.

The kind of ethos I have tried to describe in this section is as appropriate to the whole school and to the way in which everybody involved in the school interacts with each other as it is relevant to the classroom. Furthermore, I would argue that fully collaborative classrooms cannot exist unless they reflect and are reinforced by a collaborative ethos within the school.

The talking school

A student teacher in my tutorial group many years ago devised and justified as one of her assignments what she called 'The talking classroom'. As far as I recall it now, she argued for a classroom ethos focused on the power of language to activate all the humanistic qualities of thought, discussion, debate, self-expression and self-knowledge, empathy, tolerance and negotiation. The proposal was regarded at that time by the powers that be as too radical and too fanciful. I would argue that, faced with global insecurity, such a vision of schooling has become a necessity, if we are to develop in young people ways of living with others that are constructive and creative, rather than competitive and destructive. They need the support of a system that emphasizes the value of discussion and negotiation over conflict and control. Throughout this book I have aimed to demonstrate how much value is placed on discussion at all levels of the school population. But listening and talking need time, which in the current pressured ethos of schools is too often in short supply.

The humanistic school

I come to the third of the dimensions with which I have chosen to characterize the school of the 21st century. I have applied the term 'humanistic' to describe the school's function in modelling for children and young people, values, attitudes and ways of interacting that spring from the best of human motivation and achievement. We inhabit a world that is riven with conflict. We live in a pluralist, multiethnic and multicultural society. Schools can either mirror the divisions of the wider society, or they can be the nurseries for a more harmonious world. It is the responsibility of all the adults of the school and the community it serves to find a common structure of values to underpin the work of the school that everyone whatever their ethnic origin, religion or philosophy of life, can give allegiance to. Such an agreed value system will permeate relationships within the school and with parents, governors and all who interact with the school. The school will then truly belong to the community.

Education – a humanistic endeavour?

The transmission of skills, knowledge and ideas; the refinement of higher order feelings of integrity, respect and consideration, empathy, compassion, tolerance and forgiveness; the stimulation of critical thinking and creative activity; the expression of self and one's relationship to the world – all these are the province of education and educators.

It has been argued before, notably in the field of primary education (Woods *et al*, 1997) that teaching has become too instrumental, too concerned with narrowly defined achievement objectives, and that the pressures on teachers to meet attainment targets imposed by the national league tables are detracting from teachers' responsibilities for the broader goals of education. This book has attempted to make a similar argument for secondary education. Far from being concerned only with the transmission of a limited range of skills and knowledge within their specialist areas, the secondary teachers in my study reveal themselves to be concerned with the humanistic ideals of education, to foster a love of learning and a belief in the value of education for its own sake, as well as the development of mature, compassionate, imaginative and creative individuals.

Education is therefore at the heart of society, one of its defining functions, and educators at all levels are amongst its most important officers. The systemic support for teachers and teaching that I have outlined here requires first of all a commitment on the part of all sections of the community to education as an engine of change in our society, and a shared vision about the kind of society we want. Secondly, it needs resources, not the extra bits here and there, which get mostly swallowed up in increased costs, but resources that properly reflect the priority society is prepared to give to the education of its young. Those resources concern principally the provision of personnel and the creation of time.

Education and training – implications for teachers and support staff

I began this book with a quotation taken from my personal professional diary, which I wrote when I left my post as a teacher educator to return to secondary comprehensive school teaching. It documents the gap between the theory underpinning the work of teachers and the reality of classrooms in schools in difficult areas. That gap is filled by a chaotic and potentially explosive mix of frustrations and emotions as all the ideals of teaching one has built up, all the theoretical explanations for children's behaviour and achievement considered, all the stimulating teaching methods mastered and all the imaginative resources created, all fail to prevent the collapse into disorder of unmotivated and rebellious young people. If we cannot cope with the emotions of teaching we soon become stressed, demoralized and eventually burnt out. Theory provides useful explanatory frameworks for what is going on in the classroom, but it speaks to our reasoning, objective faculties. It contributes to our assessment of the situation, once we have acknowledged and learnt to deal with our feelings. Student teachers and newly qualified teachers need opportunities to come to terms with the emotions of teaching and to become sensitive to the emotions of the learners, since the battles of the classroom take place at the emotional level.

When I worked in teacher education, we had to make use of the limited periods of school experience supplemented with devised experiential learning situations, game playing and microteaching to simulate real classroom conditions. More recently, schools have been given a much greater share of the training of teachers, which now involves much more time spent in schools under the care of teacher mentors. I welcomed this change, provided that proper thought and sufficient resources were put into giving student teachers the most appropriate support and guidance. 'Pushing them in at the deep end to see if they sink or swim', is not the most helpful form of support. Early experience in the classroom needs to be structured and critiqued, not merely from the point of view of lesson content and teaching strategies, but also from the perspective of the student's feelings, the way these were being communicated and their effect on the class. Not only do students need to learn the techniques of conveying an authoritative presence, they need to learn how to deal with the emotions aroused through challenges to that authority in order to respond appropriately. This is sensitive work for the mentor, who also needs the proper time and space to conduct it effectively.

Newly qualified teachers, teachers new to the school, returners to the profession and all support and ancillary staff who come into routine contact with groups of children and young people need this supported space to deal with their own emotions before their behaviour becomes distorted. Only adults who are in control of their own feelings and know how to express these constructively are in a position to support and guide young people through the often painful emotions of growing up.

It may be argued that schools have enough to do to fulfil their main function of educating and developing young people, and cannot also undertake the job training and professional development of all their staff. I like the concept of the learning community, which in recent years has entered the vocabulary of professional training in a number of spheres. At present there is a them and us ethos in schools. *We*, the teachers, know; we teach *them*, the pupils. But we are all in the business of both teaching and learning, and schools as formal learning institutions should be pioneers in modelling new frameworks for continuing education and lifelong learning relevant to the function of the school.

Conclusion

In my introduction, I warned that readers who expected a manual of point by point advice and instruction on how to support teachers or pupils would be disappointed by this book. I hope I have been able to show that the issues surrounding support are too complex to be reduced to a list of dos and don'ts. What I have tried to do is to explore through my conversations with teachers, support staff and pupils in one school, backed by my own experience and reading, the principles on which effective support provisions for teachers might be based. From their own testimonies, teachers want conditions in which they can teach according to their own professional values and purposes. Failure to be the teachers they want to be creates enormous emotional pressures, which may ultimately lead to distorted behaviour in the classroom. Secondary school teachers see their task as a dual one of

communicating their subject in exciting and motivating ways, and of catering for the individual needs, academic, social and personal, of their pupils.
One of the obstacles to fulfilling this dual role is the difficulty of coping with
the behaviour of pupils. But pupils also experience considerable emotional
conflict in the classroom between their desire to conform to teachers' expectations and their need to conform to the demands of the peer group. Much
classroom confrontation is the result of the clash of emotions emanating
from the misperceptions of both teacher and pupils about the intentions and
attitudes of the other.

Both teachers and pupils want humanistic classroom conditions, which
allow each to behave towards the other with respect and to work purposively.
Support is ideally directed at providing the attitudes, structures and facilities
for this to happen. Support will be directed at the emotional needs of the
classroom as well as the practical needs.

Support involves a rethinking of attitudes towards teachers who need help.
It should be seen as a right and a necessity to allow harmonious and
collaborative classrooms to exist, rather than as a prop for teachers who
cannot cope on their own. All the support initiatives discussed in Part II of
this book are evaluated according to these principles.

Support is not confined to providing help in the immediate situation.
As teachers themselves agreed, support also consists in helping teachers to
extend their range of skills and to critically reflect on their work, provided
that teachers themselves are involved in determining their own needs and
the directions they want to take in developing their work. Examples of the
kinds of professional training that teachers find helpful and relevant have
been included. Above all, teachers need the trust of society to allow them to
determine what is best for their school, their pupils and themselves. That is
what professionalism is for.

Without institutional, community and societal support, teachers will continue to become too demoralized to make the changes to our education
system which children and young people clearly need, if they are to become
less alienated. These changes, however, cannot be the knee-jerk reactions to
the perceived crises in schools we have seen in the last three decades. A fundamental reappraisal, which involves us all, is needed of the role of schools and
schooling in the 21st century. Support for teachers cannot, however, wait
until society has determined its priorities. Every school, every local authority
can start evaluating now its attitudes to teachers and the kinds of institutional
support provided. Our teachers and their pupils deserve nothing less.

Appendix

The structure of Eastbank School's Assertive Discipline System

Reward systems

1 *Academic*. Pupils receive stars, stickers or smiley faces for good or improved work, which accumulate to earn merit checks. The precise structure of the system for each subject is determined within subject departments.
2 *Service*. Pupils receive service checks for helpful or socially responsible actions at the discretion of the teacher.
3 *Classroom behaviour under the Assertive Discipline System* (positive consequences). Pupils begin each lesson with a credit for attendance at the lesson. If they complete the lesson without incurring penalties for inappropriate behaviour according to the rules of the classroom (see below) they retain their credit. These accumulate in multiples of 10 to earn progressively three certificates. Attainment of the third stage certificate entitles the pupil to enter a prize draw at the end of term.

Classroom rules

These are common to the whole school, agreed by staff and discussed with parents and pupils before the introduction of the ADS. They may be modified or added to through agreement with subject departments to meet the needs of specific subject teaching:

1 Come to lessons properly equipped.
2 Enter quietly and wait for lesson to begin.
3 Obey the teacher's instructions without fuss.
4 Stay in your seat unless given permission to do otherwise. No wandering around the room.

5   Raise your hand. Do not shout out. No calling out to friends.
6   Do not chew, eat or drink during lessons.
7   Treat the teacher and each other, and other people's property with respect.

Negative consequences

Pupils incur penalties for inappropriate behaviour in a lesson according to the following scale:

1   At the first infringement the pupil's name is written on the board, and she or he loses the automatic credit. This also constitutes a warning. (The system was later modified to allow teachers to issue a reminder or warning before the loss of credit.)
2   A second infringement results in a half-break detention.
3   A third infringement results in a full-break detention.
4   A fourth infringement results in an after school detention, where parents are given 24 hours' notice.
5   Persistent bad behaviour beyond this point results in exclusion to the remove room.
6   Persistent attendance in the remove room may result in procedures for suspension being initiated.

The 'extreme' clause

Teachers may send a pupil to the remove room immediately in an emergency or for extremely bad behaviour, without activating the normal scale of sanctions.

The remove room

This is staffed by senior and middle management on a timetabled basis. Pupils are normally required to remain in the remove room for a minimum of seven lesson periods (a complete school day) from the time of referral; or until parents have been contacted by the head of the subject department and have come into the school to discuss the matter. Folders of tasks for each subject area are available in the remove room.

Senior staff on-call rota

This allows for a member of the senior management team to be available at all times to respond to calls from class teachers for immediate assistance when necessary.

Record-keeping

The system requires detailed record-keeping by subject class teachers of both credits and negative consequences. Detentions are recorded on slips, which are then entered onto the computer. This allows for a complete record of a pupil's behaviour across the school. It also allows access to the sanctioning patterns of teachers, theoretically indicating where support may be required. Subject departments also have their own record-keeping arrangements so that the head of department has oversight of pupil behaviour and teachers' classroom management within the department.

References and additional reading

Bainer, D and Didham, C (1994) 'Mentoring and other support behaviors in elementary schools', *Journal of Educational Research*, **87** (4), March/April, 240–47.

BERA (2002), British Educational Research Association, Annual Conference, Exeter.

Blandford, S (1998) *Managing Discipline in Schools*, London, Routledge.

Canter, L and Canter, M (1992) *Lee Canter's Assertive Discipline*, Santa Monica, Lee Canter and Associates.

Carlyle, D and Woods, P (2002) *Emotions of Teacher Stress*, Stoke-on-Trent, Trentham Books.

Chisholm, B (1994) 'Promoting peer support among teachers', in Gray, Miller and Noakes (eds).

Coldron, J (2002) 'We just talk things through and then she helps me', unpublished paper, British Educational Research Association Conference (BERA).

Cole, M and Walker, S (eds) (1989) *Teaching and Stress*, Milton Keynes, Open University.

Creese, A, Norwich, B and Daniels, H (1997a) 'Provision of a teacher-centred strategy for implementing the Code of Practice', unpublished report, Institute of Education, University of London.

Creese, A, Norwich, B and Daniels, H (1997b) *Teacher Support Teams in Secondary Schools*, London, Department for Education and Employment.

Cronk, K A (1987) *Teacher–Pupil Conflict in Secondary Schools*, Lewes, Falmer.

Dunham, J (1992) *Stress in Teaching*, London, Routledge.

Elton, Lord (1989) *Discipline in Schools*, London, HMSO.

Faupel, A, Herrick, E and Sharp, P (1998), *Anger Management: a Practical Guide*, London, David Fulton.

Galvin, P and Costa, P (1994) 'Building better behaved schools: effective support at the whole school level', in Gray, Miller and Noakes (eds).

Gewirz, S (1996) 'Post-welfarism and the reconstruction of teachers' work', unpublished paper, British Educational Research Association Annual Conference (BERA).

Gillborn, D A, Nixon, J and Ruddock, J (1993) *Dimensions of Discipline*, London, HMSO.

Goleman, D (1995) *Emotional Intelligence*, London, Bloomsbury.

Goleman, D (1998) *Working with Emotional Intelligence*, London, Bloomsbury.

Gray, P, Miller, A and Noakes, J (1994) *Challenging Behaviour in Schools*, London, Routledge.

Hanko, G (1995) *Special Needs in Ordinary Classrooms*, London, David Fulton.

Hargreaves, A (1994) *Changing Teachers, Changing Times: Teachers' Work and Culture in the Postmodern Age*, London, Cassell.

Hargreaves, D (1994) *The Mosaic of learning*, London, Demos.

Hodkinson, P (2002) 'Improving incentives for workplace learning', unpublished paper, presented at the British Educational Research Association (BERA) Conference.

Kinder, K, Wakefield, A and Wilkin, A (1996) *Talking Back, Pupil Views on Disaffection*, Slough, NFER.

Kyriakou, C (1989) 'The nature and prevalence of stress in teaching', in Cole and Walker.

Measor, L and Woods, P (1984) *Changing Schools*, Milton Keynes, Open University.

Nelson, B S (1986) 'Collaboration for colleagueship: a program in support of teachers', *Educational Leadership*, **43** (5), 50–52.

Nias, J (1989) *Primary Teachers Talking*, London, Routledge.

Prior, D and Wilson, J (1994) 'Support in secondary schools: a complex problem', in Gray, Millar and Noakes (eds).

Rutter, M, Maughan, B, Mortimore, P, Ouston, J and Smith, A (1979) *Fifteen Thousand Hours*, London, Open Books.

Sharp, P ( ) *Nurturing Emotional Literacy: a Practical Guide for Teachers, Parents and Those in the Caring Professions*, London, David Fulton.

Showers, B and Joyce, B (1996) 'The evolution of peer coaching', *Educational Leadership*, **53** (6) 12–16.

Travers, C J and Cooper, C L (1996) *Teachers under Pressure*, London, Routledge.

Wheldall, K and Merrett, F (1984) *Positive Teaching, the Behavioural Approach*, London, George, Allen and Unwin.

Wilson, D (2001) 'Teacher support: an exploration of the concept of teacher support, investigating how secondary comprehensive school teachers perceive their classroom needs and define the support required to fulfil their professional role', unpublished PhD thesis, Leeds Metropolitan University.

Woodhead, C (1997), reported in Carvel, J 'Crackdown on bad teachers', *The Guardian*, 16 July 1997.

Woodhead, C (2002) *Class war: The State of British Education*, London, Little, Brown.

Woods, P (1979) *The Divided School*, London, Routledge and Kegan Paul.

Woods, P (1990) *Teacher Skills and Strategies*, Basingstoke, Falmer.

Woods, P and Jeffrey, R (1996) 'A new professional discourse?' in Woods (ed.), *Contemporary Issues in Teaching and Learning*, London, Routledge/Open University.

Woods, P, Jeffrey, R, Troman, G and Boyle, M (1997) *Restructuring Schools, Reconstructing Teachers: Responding to Change in the Primary School*, Buckingham, Open University Press.

Index